Warrior • 33

Knight Hospitaller (1)

1100–1306

David Nicolle · Illustrated by Christa Hook

271.7912
Nic

First published in Great Britain in 2001 by Osprey Publishing,
Midland House, West Way, Botley, Oxford OX2 0PH, UK
443 Park Avenue South, New York, NY 10016, USA
Email: info@ospreypublishing.com

CIP Data for this publication is available from the British Library

ISBN-10: 1-84176-214-8
ISBN-13: 978-1-84176-214-2

Editor: Nikolai Bogdanovic
Design: The Black Spot
Index by Alan Rutter
Originated by Magnet Harlequin, Uxbridge, UK
Typeset in Helvetica Neue and ITC New Baskerville
Printed in China through World Print Ltd.

06 07 08 09 10 14 13 12 11 10 9 8 7 6 5

FOR A CATALOGUE OF ALL BOOKS PUBLISHED BY
OSPREY MILITARY AND AVIATION PLEASE CONTACT:

NORTH AMERICA
Osprey Direct, C/o Random House Distribution
Center, 400 Hahn Road, Westminster, MD 21157, USA
E-mail: info@ospreydirect.com

ALL OTHER REGIONS
Osprey Direct UK, P.O. Box 140, Wellingborough,
Northants, NN8 2FA, UK
E-mail: info@ospreydirect.co.uk

www.ospreypublishing.com

Artist's note

Readers may care to note that the original paintings from
which the colour plates in this book were prepared are
available for private sale. All reproduction copyright
whatsoever is retained by the Publishers. All enquiries
should be addressed to:

Scorpio Gallery, PO Box 475,
Hailsham, East Sussex, BN27 2SL, UK.

The Publishers regret that they can enter into no
correspondence upon this matter.

Dedication

For my cousin, Juliet McPhearson-Heard, who wanted to
help the sick (died Hither Green 5 November 1967).

KNIGHT HOSPITALLER (1)
1100–1306

A biblical figure, perhaps Abraham, in the garb of a pilgrim or travelling monk on a carved capital, Burgundian 1120-30. (In situ Cathedral, Autun, France; author's photograph)

INTRODUCTION: 'WARRIOR MONKS'

Unlike their sometime rivals the Templars, the Order of St John of the Hospital of Jerusalem (or the Hospitallers as they are better known) was not created as a result of the First Crusade in 1099. It already existed, but the way in which the Order then evolved from a charitable organisation into one of the most effective fighting forces of the Middle Ages was a consequence of the crusading movement. In the process the Hospitallers became recognised experts in the military capabilities of opposing Islamic armies. As their military importance grew, so the Military Orders asserted increasing independence in matters of war and peace with neighbouring peoples. The failure of the Crusader States to expand after their first few successful years also meant that they lacked sufficient land to maintain adequate armies. In fact these largely urban coastal states often relied on mercenaries and, of course, the dedicated standing armies of the Military Orders.

While the Hospitallers increased in power and influence in the Middle East, so the system of financial and logistical support which they created in Western Europe similarly grew in size, wealth and political influence. The Hospitaller presence in Western Europe was largely non-military, with the major exception of their role in the Iberian peninsula. Here, on what could be called Latin Christendom's second front with the Islamic world, the Hospitallers and other Military Orders took a leading part in the Spanish Reconquista. But even here, the *ifrir*, as they were known to their Muslim Moorish opponents (from the French *frères* or brothers), were not singled out for the special attention given them in the Middle East.

CHRONOLOGY

c. 1080	Establishment of the Hospital of St John in Jerusalem under Islamic rule.
1099	First Crusade captures Jerusalem; the Blessed Gerard traditionally becomes the first Master of the Order of St John of Jerusalem.
1113	Pope Paschal II recognises the Hospital of St John in Jerusalem as an Order of the Church; the Blessed Gerard becomes actual first Master.
1119-20	Order of the Knights Templar founded.
1120	Death of the Blessed Gerard; the Blessed Raymond du Puy becomes Master of the order.
1126	First reference to a *constable* of the Hospitallers.
1128	Order of the Templars officially recognised by the Catholic Church.
c. 1130	Composition of the first *Rule* of the Order of Hospitallers.
c. 1135-54	Hospitallers awarded exemption, becoming independent of local religious authorities.

1136	Castle of Bethgibelin granted to Hospitallers.	
1144	Krak des Chevaliers and four smaller castles given to the Hospitallers.	
1147-48	First unclear reference to a brother-knight of the Hospitallers.	
***c.* 1150**	Construction of Hospitaller castle at Belmont.	
1160	Auger de Balben becomes Master of the order.	
1162	Arnold de Comps becomes Master of the order, followed by Gilbert d'Assailly the same year.	
1163-69	Definite emergence of Hospitaller brothers-in-arms.	
1168-72	Construction of Hospitaller castle of Belvoir.	
1170	Cast de Murols becomes Master of the order.	
1172	Jobert de Syrie becomes Master of the order.	
1177	Roger de Moulins becomes Master of the order; Crusader States defeat Saladin at Mont Gisard.	
1186	Castle of Marqab given to the Hospitallers.	
1187	Saladin crushes kingdom of Jerusalem at battle of Hattin; Armengaud d'Asp becomes Master of the order; Saladin retakes Jerusalem and Hospitallers lose their HQ.	
1188	Rule written for the Hospitaller Sisters in Aragon.	
1190	Garnier de Naples becomes Master of the order.	
1191	Hospitallers move their headquarters to Acre.	
1193	Geoffrey de Donjon becomes Master of the order.	
1202	Severe earthquake damages Krak des Chevaliers, after which Hospitallers decide on major enlargement.	
1203	Alfonso de Portugal becomes Master of the order.	
1206	Geoffrey le Rat becomes Master of the order.	
1207	Garin de Montaigu becomes Master of the order.	
1228	Bertrand de Thessy becomes Master of the order.	
1229	Jerusalem ceded to the Kingdom of Jerusalem by treaty; Hospitaller HQ remains in Acre.	
1230	Guerin becomes Master of the order.	
1236	Bertrand de Comps becomes Master of the order.	
1239	Pierre de Vieille Bride becomes Master of the order.	
1242	Guillaume de Châteauneuf becomes Master of the order.	
1244	Jerusalem retaken by Muslims (Khwarazmians).	
1256-58	Civil war in kingdom of Jerusalem.	
1258	Hugues Revel becomes Master of the order.	
1263-68	Mamluks devastate Nazareth, retake Caesarea, Arsuf, Saphet, Jaffa, Belfort and Antioch.	
1271	Mamluks retake Chastel Blanc, Krak des Chevaliers and Montfort.	
1274	Proposal to unify all Military Orders is not adopted.	
1277-83	Civil war in County of Tripoli (1277-83).	
1285	Jean de Villiers becomes Master of the order; Mamluks take Marqab.	
1287-89	Mamluks retake Latakia and Tripoli.	
1291	Mamluks retake Acre; almost all remaining Crusader enclaves taken or abandoned.	
1293	Eudes des Pins becomes Master of the order.	
1296	Guillaume de Villaret becomes Master of the order.	
1299	Mamluks take castle of Roche Guillaume.	
1302	Mamluks take Ruad island; probable end of Latin authority in Jbayl.	
1305	Foulques de Villaret becomes Master of the order.	
1306	Hospitallers begin invasion of Byzantine island of Rhodes.	

RIGHT **The Citadel of Antioch looking down the near vertical line of the northern walls to the city below. The Order of the Hospitallers owned some properties in Antioch, but transferred them to other owners. (Author's photograph)**

ORIGINS AND MILITARISATION OF THE HOSPITALLERS

The Hospital of St John in Jerusalem existed well before the First Crusade was launched in 1095, having been founded or revived by a group of Italian merchants from Amalfi in the mid-11th century as part of a widespread charitable movement to help pilgrims. By the 1080s it was a flourishing organisation under the patronage of the Latin Church of Santa Maria Latina south of the great Church of the Holy Sepulchre. Here, secular people lived a quasi-religious life and tended the sick. Two hospices, were established, one for female pilgrims and another for men.

Following the capture of Jerusalem by the First Crusade, most crusaders returned home, leaving the newly established Crusader States of Jerusalem, Tripoli, Antioch and Edessa seriously short of troops. Fortunately for the new states it also took many years for the neighbouring Islamic countries to overcome their chronic fragmentation and begin to fight back effectively. During these the early years the Hospital of St John remained a medical organisation. It developed under the leadership of the Blessed Gerard who had probably been the guardian of the original hospital before the arrival of the crusader invaders, and had remained in the city during their siege. French influence replaced that of the Italians and the Hospital won wider support. The buildings were extended and by the time of Gerard's death in 1120 the Hospitallers had been freed from supervision by the Benedictines monks of Santa Maria Latina and even by the Church of the Holy Sepulchre. They became, in effect, an autonomous religious

ABOVE **The primitive, and now very battered, wall-paintings in Hardham date from around 1125. In addition to a picture of St George slaying a Muslim at Antioch there is this illustration of King Herod's guards in which the wicked ruler's soldiers have been given Middle Eastern lamellar armour. (In situ, Church of St Botolph, Hardham, England; author's photograph)**

The fortified Greek Orthodox Monastery of St George stands in the shadow of the huge Hospitaller castle of Krak des Chevaliers. The Mamluk sultan permitted it to remain when the castle was conquered. (Author's photograph)

institution unlike any other religious hospital in Latin Christendom and eventually the Order took control of most other hospitals within the Crusader States. Quite when the Hospitallers started to establish hospitals in Europe is unclear, though the first to appear north of the Alps was probably at Utrecht which dated from 1122. The Hospitallers also created a support service across Western Europe based upon a network of *commanderies* and *baillies* whose primary function was to provide funds, materials and recruits for the Order in the Holy Land.

The Templars were founded as a military organisation to defend pilgrims, but the Hospitallers only gradually became involved in such activities some time before 1160. To many in the modern Western world the idea of 'warrior monks' seems a contradiction in terms. Most medieval people thought differently and many Christian scholars believed that violence was necessary to maintain justice or to impose peace. Some wars came to be seen as a remedy for sin rather than as a consequence of it, and the slaughter of wrongdoers and non-Christians became regarded as an 'act of love'. The ethos of the early Crusades also declared Muslims to be *summa culpabilis*, the 'most blameworthy' of people.

Though some clergymen questioned the validity of officially recognised Military Orders, the Papacy recognised their usefulness. All agreed, however, that brethren of the Military Orders earned less 'spiritual merit' than did the traditional and contemplative monastic orders. Once their effectiveness had been demonstrated, the Military Orders came to be seen by the rulers of the Crusader States as more reliable contingents than the uncertain and often insubordinate feudal troops or paid mercenaries. On the other hand, the presence of Hospitaller brethren on a battlefield does not prove they were there to fight. Documents record the donation of military equipment to the Order before 1143, but these could have been for armed servants of the Order. Nevertheless, Hospitallers were soon involved in the division of spoils after a campaign and in the mid-1130s King Fulk of Jerusalem gave the Hospitallers Bayt Jibrin where they built a castle known as Bethgibelin. Other strategic locations soon followed, and military men attached themselves to an Order which was becoming a potent military force. Then came the catastrophe of 1187 when Saladin defeated the main field army of the Crusader States and recaptured not only Jerusalem but most crusader territory as well. Not surprisingly, the Papacy now supported the dedicated Military Orders to an even greater extent while encouraging further Crusades from the West.

RECRUITMENT

During the 12th century those who went on Crusade normally had to be free men. If they were serfs they had to obtain manumission from their lords and be able to cover their own expenses. The only real exception were the *ministeriales* of Germany who technically remained serfs while gradually evolving into a knightly class. The Military Orders recruited from the same classes. Casualties meant that men were constantly needed and many, particularly in France, wanted to join the Hospitallers. Yet their numbers were constantly limited by the Order's shortage of money. Men sent to the Middle East tended to be the fit and relatively young, while older members of the Order generally remained in Europe, running a fast expanding support network.

France remained the powerhouse of the crusading movement and provided the bulk of Hospitaller personnel. England was in many ways a cultural colony of France, yet it played a significant role in the Order

The Hospitallers held the now abandoned village of Bugaea (Khirbat Bakha) near Jisr al-Majami on the River Jordan as well as many others in this area. (Author's photograph)

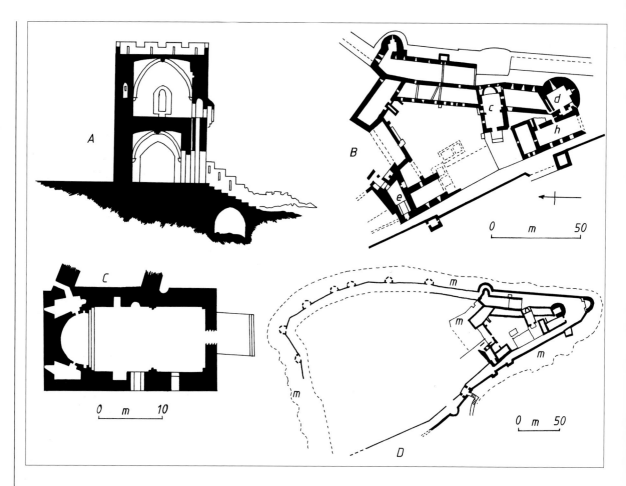

The Hospitaller castle at Marqab on the Syrian coast. A: section through entrance-tower (e) showing overhanging machicolation, groove for portcullis and a guard-room above. B: plan of the castle; c - chapel; d - donjon, keep; e - entrance tower; h - hall. C: chapel in Marqab castle. D: plan of the castle and fortified town; m - dry moat.

during the 12th century. Very large numbers of troops were available in the German Empire, but here and in German-dominated regions of Central Europe, recruitment for the Hospitallers and Templars faced stiff competition from a locally based Order – the Teutonic Knights. In fact, there was reluctance to join the Templars who were considered too French and too close to the Papacy at a time when the German emperors and the popes were often at loggerheads. The Hospitallers faced less of a problem and recruited widely in Bohemia where most of the senior Hospitallers were German. The Order also flourished in the sprawling kingdom of Hungary, but here again most of the leading men were French or Italian, while ordinary brethren were Hungarian, Croats or German settlers. Hospitallers of Croatian and Bosnian origin served in Italy which was itself something of a special case. Like Germany, Italy had abundant well-trained professional soldiers but they tended to have local loyalties rather than joining the Military Orders. The Iberian peninsula was again different. Enthusiasm for holy war was strong, but it focused on the local frontier with Moorish-Islamic Andalusia. Most senior Hospitallers in Spain or Portugal were also of local origin.

During the 12th and 13th centuries brethren of the Hospitaller Order of St John were not recruited solely from the nobility. After the 1260s, however, preference was given to those of knightly rank who brought with them larger financial donations, and thereafter the restrictions on recruitment gradually became more rigorous. During the

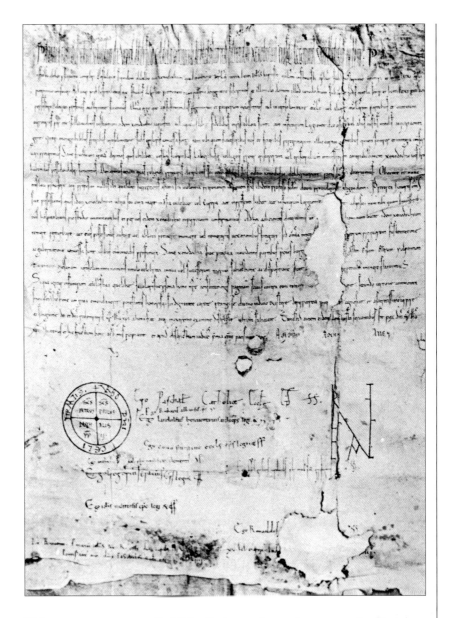

12th century systems of child *oblation* and attachment to the Order as *novitiates* were more important than in later years. *Novitiates* also included abandoned children who were not, however, obliged to join once they came of age. In some other orders a *novitiate* became a full brother at 14 or 15 after three years training, but in later years high casualties and the demand for men who were already trained soldiers probably accounted for a decline in the *novitiate* system. On the other hand, the absence of a proper *novitiate* system led to widespread illiteracy among recruits and frequent breaches in regulations which were not fully understood.

Very little is known about the motivation of individual recruits. The life of a Hospitaller brother may have looked relatively easy to someone on the outside: there were career prospects and joining a Military Order meant less 'abandonment of the world' than joining a regular monastic order. Some recruits may actually have been looking for martyrdom in

Mount Tabor was believed to be the site of Christ's Transfiguration and the Crusaders built a castle here to protect pilgrims. This was handed to the Hospitallers in 1255. (Author's photograph)

A carved capital in the church at Mozac in central France provides a simple but remarkably accurate illustration of a fully armed knight from around 1160. (In situ Abbey Church of St Calmin, Mozac, France; author's photograph)

war at a time of genuine religious conviction, but in the late 13th century a few were trying to escape debts or legal punishment although criminals or debtors were barred by the Order's rules.

The qualifications required of a recruit to the Hospitallers were clear. There was no lower age limit, although there were rules about when a man could become a knight or be ordained a priest. All recruits had to be free, of legitimate birth, healthy, spiritually clean and not in debt. During the 13th century a brother-knight had to be of knightly descent and most came from the lower aristocracy. Married men were only accepted if their living spouses agreed, and sometimes man and wife joined together. Men were expected to be fit enough to fight, though standards dropped in times of crisis. Ex-members of other Orders were not accepted, and Hospitallers were similarly not permitted to leave once they joined. When individuals managed to buy their way past these regulations, such simony caused considerable scandal.

The entry procedure was simple and solemn, the recruit being warned that, 'although it may be that you see us well-clothed and with fine horses, and think that we have every comfort, you would be mistaken, for when you would like to eat it will be necessary to fast. And when you want to sleep it will be necessary to keep watch.' During the Sunday chapter (meeting) of a convent a prospective recruit asked the Master of the order or the presiding brother for membership. If the majority of the chapter agreed, the candidate was asked if he fulfilled the basic entry requirements; if he was later found to have lied he would be expelled. The candidate then placed his hands on a missal or mass book and took an oath to God, Our Lady and St John the Baptist, stating that he would live and die in obedience to the sovereign given him by God – in effect the Master of the order – in chastity, without property, a serf and slave of 'his lords the sick'. At the end of the ceremony the president held up the basic costume of the Order and said, 'Behind this, the sign of the Cross which you will wear on this mantle in remembrance of Him who suffered death and passion on the Cross for you and for us other sinners. May God, by the Cross and by the vow of obedience that you have made in faith and in deed, keep you and defend you now and for ever, from the power of the Devil.' After the mantle was placed upon the new brother's shoulder he was given the Kiss of Peace which he then exchanged with all brethren present.

Numbers of recruits varied over the years and, despite its proverbial wealth, the Order of the Hospital could not afford to maintain as many fighting men or as many castles as it might have wished. In the early days any Hospitaller commander could accept a knight as a recruit, though only the Master or a specially designated brother could accept a sergeant. In 1270 it was decided that the authority of the Master was needed before the commanders of Cyprus, Tripoli and Armenia could create new brethren, although the commanders and chapters of larger establishments at Acre, Krak des Chevaliers and Marqab could still accept recruits. In 1292, after the fall of Acre, the Hospitallers' finances were even more strained and so no new brothers could be created anywhere except in Spain without a specific licence from the Master or Grand Commander.

The case of brother-sergeants was different. In the earliest years there were no brother-knights or brother-sergeants – all were merely brothers. After the brother-sergeants emerged as a distinct group in the early 13th century their numbers remained lower than the knights, despite the division between brother-sergeants-at-arms or *caravaniers*, who were soldiers, and brother-sergeants-at-service who undertook menial or administrative tasks. They still led the same conventual or communal way of life, but were often given considerable responsibility. The brother-sergeants must not be confused with a much larger number

Several villages in northern Jordan were listed as belonging to the Hospitallers. One was Bayt Ras, known to the Crusaders as Beteras, where the ruins of early medieval shops have been discovered by archaeologists. (Author's photograph)

of ordinary sergeants, who were merely servants of the Order. Details about the backgrounds of the brother-sergeants remain very obscure, but most seem to have been of peasant or artisan origin; there were cases of men from knightly families joining as brother-sergeants, perhaps because they had not yet been knighted. As a religious order, the Hospitallers needed their own priests, although the first reference to such a clerical brother only dates from 1154. In fact, the Hospitallers continued to face difficulty recruiting priests and many convents relied on outsiders to serve their religious needs.

On the margins of the Order of the Hospitallers were a variety of other groups, including the *donats*, noblemen who wanted to join as full brethren but had to wait in a sort of queue after going to the Holy Land at their own expense. *Confraters* were laymen, often of high noble rank, who were associated with the Hospitallers but did not normally become brethren. They had agreed to defend a Hospitaller convent or house and were given a status in a simple religious ceremony. During the 13th century a separate Confraternity of St George and St Belian was established for Christians of the Melkite Syrian Church which was in communion with Rome.

The backbone of Hospitaller power was financial rather than numerical and by the late 12th century the Order held large territories in the Crusader States and Europe. Their feudal fiefs in the Middle East supposedly contributed knights and other troops to the Hospitaller muster, but the reliability of their vassals seems to have been questionable, especially as many of the peasants were Muslims. Other indigenous troops played a more significant role in Hospitaller forces, including the famous Turcopoles, but they were not, of course, brethren of the Order. The Hospitallers similarly enlisted Western European mercenaries and servants in the early 13th century, but again, they were not members of the Order.

Another village claimed by the Order of the Hospitallers was Qadmus in the Syrian mountains. It was retaken by the Muslims in 1131 but the Hospitallers still forced Qadmus and two neighbouring castles to pay tribute in the 13th century. (Author's photograph)

RIGHT The Hospitaller castle of Belvoir overlooks the River Jordan. Its concentric design reflects the fact that it was a monastic enclosure as well as a castle. (Author's photograph)

ORGANISATION AND STRUCTURE

The militarisation of the Hospitallers was followed by a period when several of its masters were of Anglo-Norman origin. The first was Gilbert d'Assailly who was elected in 1162 and had previously been the Commander at Tyre. Under his mastership the militarisation of the Hospitallers gathered pace. The last of the Anglo-Norman masters was a confidant of the crusading King Richard I, Garnier de Naples, who died 1192. The Hospitallers' first headquarters had been in Jerusalem but following Saladin's liberation of the holy city in 1187 and the Third Crusade's subsequent recapture of the Palestinian coast, they moved to Acre. The Order's main military effort was, however, concentrated further north where it acquired a quasi-independent and strategically located territory around the great castles of Krak des Chevaliers and Marqab.

Some Hospitallers managed to spend almost their entire careers in the Middle East, but there was also some form of troop rotation in which individual members of the Order did one tour of duty in the Holy Land. Only a small proportion of the Hospitaller personnel were actually stationed in the region. Many more, including brothers-in-arms, remained in Europe. This strategic reserve was so widely spread that Western convents outside Spain contained, at most, a handful of properly equipped fighting men. Hospitallers in the west were largely non-military sergeants who controlled the Order's increasingly large estates and wealth. This was also true of Hospitaller convents in Central

ABOVE **The Hospitallers attracted men from everywhere in Catholic Christendom, including Croatia. This 12th century Croatian manuscript shows the military costume of what was then a frontier region of Latin Christendom. (Missal, Metropolitan Library, Ms. MR.138, Zagreb, Croatia)**

The interiors of some of the main Hospitaller castles were decorated with wall paintings. This picture of a baptism came from the chapel in Krak des Chevaliers. (Historical Museum, Tartus, Syria)

and Eastern Europe, and it was only after the devastating Mongol invasions of Hungary in the 13th century that more than a handful of brother-knights were stationed in this frontier kingdom of Latin Christendom. Hospitaller organisation in the Iberian peninsula mirrored that in the Middle East, and Hospitaller possessions were mostly concentrated on the flanks of the frontier with the Islamic south.

Ranks and hierarchy

Ranks within the Order of the Hospitallers reflected status and function, with brother-knights and brother-sergeants having essentially the same military equipment, although that of the sergeants tended to be more limited. In the earliest days there had not even been a clear division between brothers-at-arms and non-military brothers-at-service, but by the 13th century the brethren formed four main groups: the knights or brother-knights-at-arms, the brother-sergeants-at-arms, the non-military brothers-in-office and the smaller number of chaplains or priests. The most important division was, in fact, between the ordained priests and the ordinary brethren. However, class divisions between brother-knights and brother-sergeants hardened during the 13th century, while those of illegitimate birth were only allowed limited authority by the late 13th century. From 1262 only a brother-knight could become Master and by 1320, brother-knights even took precedence over priests.

The most important official in the Order of the Hospitallers was, of course, the **Master** who was elected by committee, served for the rest of his life, and had his own household and servants. The **Grand Commander** was the master's administrative second-in-command, responsible for supplies, domestic administration, the Order's Middle Eastern properties and the Central Convent in Palestine when the Master was absent. By 1303 the vital *arbalestry* (crossbow-store) was one of his *bailiwicks* (areas of responsibility).

The **Marshal** was the most senior military official in the Order, responsible for discipline in the Central Convent where he was regarded as the men's leader; the Grand Commander was seen as the Master's representative. Following a military restructuring of the Order in 1206, all brothers-in-arms were placed under his authority. He continued to distribute military equipment and horses, being in charge of the forge and saddlery, as well as issuing rations and clothing to those sent on missions away from the Convent. On campaign the Marshal commanded Hospitaller forces under the immediate authority of the Master or his lieutenant, and led the field army if the Master was absent. In fact all military officers in the Middle East were under the Marshal to some extent, the only exceptions being the *capitular* (senior) *bailli* and the Master's own companions. Lesser military officers such as the master esquire, gonfanier (standard-bearer) and commander of the knights were under the marshal, as were almost all castellans after 1303, along with the Turcopolier in time of war and the admiral if the marshal himself was with the fleet.

As the second most senior *conventual bailli* after the Grand Commander, the Marshal reported directly to the General Chapter (governing committee) of the Order. The marshal's standard-bearer was in fact the **Gonfanier** of the Order as a whole. Since 1206 he had been permitted four horses, two squires, two pack animals and one driver. A

This panel from a wooden doorway came from a church in Lebanon and might date from the late 13th or perhaps early 14th century Crusader period. (Formerly Pharaon Collection, Beirut, present whereabouts unknown)

regulation of 1268 specified that the Marshal was allowed a turcoman, hack or riding horse in addition to his destrier or warhorse, though this had to be made available if a brother-in-arms needed it in battle.

As the Hospitallers' senior military figure, the Marshal was widely consulted for his expertise on Middle Eastern affairs. Nevertheless, his power was offset by the fact that those holding this office changed so often. Military equipment donated to the Order went to the Marshal's office unless it had been specifically given to the castles of Krak des Chevaliers or Marqab. Furthermore, the Marshal could requisition such items from local commanders. The *marshalsy* itself had two main departments: the arsenal where at least one brother-in-arms looked after all military equipment except crossbows, and the stables which faced a perpetual shortage of horses and a chronic wastage of animals shipped from Europe.

The **Constable** was a senior military officer, though his responsibilities were organisational and he remained subordinate to the marshal until 1169. The position of **Master Esquire** of the Central Convent dated from the military reorganisation of 1206. Responsible for squires and grooms and for supervising work concerning the horses and stables, he was the immediate superior of the *crie, acrie* or *cria* who actually ran the stables, issuing mounts and possibly harnesses to brothers-in-arms. The role of Master Esquire was given to one of the most senior or experienced brother-sergeants, but he should not be confused with another master esquire who led the Master's own squires and was later called the **Grand Esquire**.

The position of **Gonfanonier**, or standard bearer, of the Order seems to have been offered as a reward for skill or courage in battle. He was

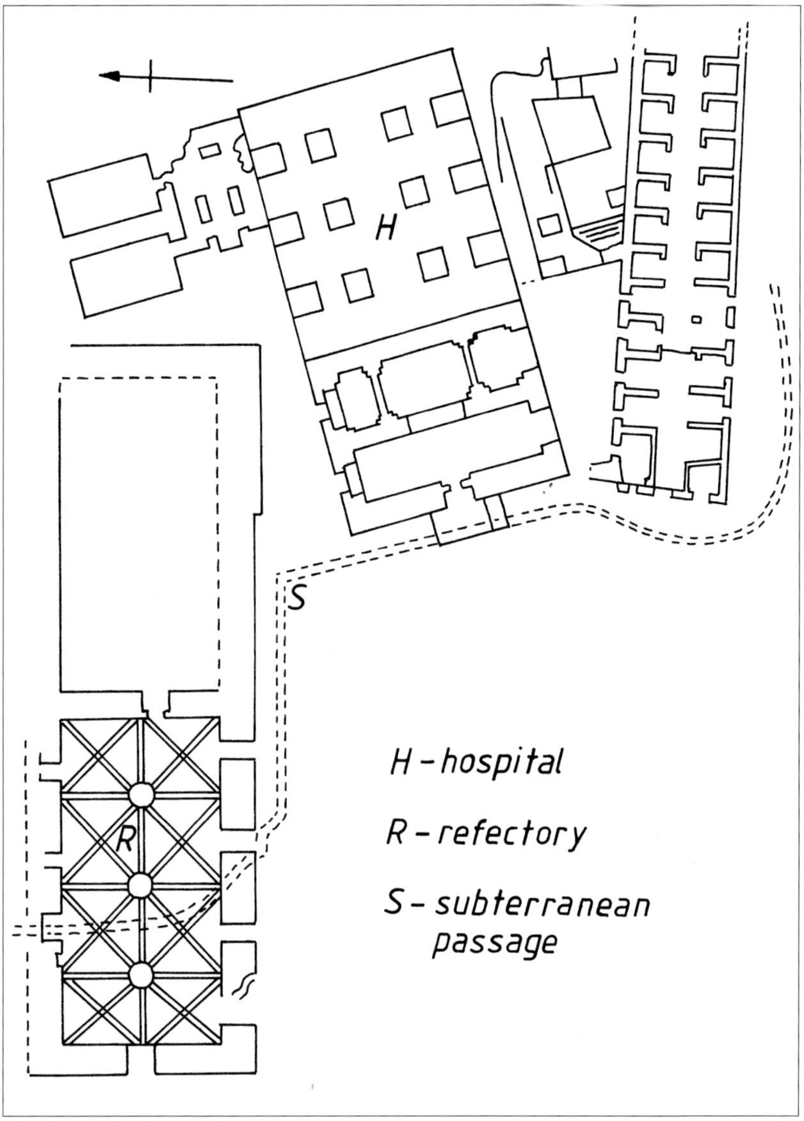

The Hospitaller complex in Acre in Palestine as excavated by archaeologists in the 1960s (after Z. Goldmann).

H – hospital

R – refectory

S – subterranean passage

put beneath the Marshal following the reorganisation of 1206, and from 1270 had to be a brother-knight of legitimate birth. The Gonfanonier could also lead raids if the Master, his lieutenant or the Marshal were not available. The Commander of Knights actually led the knights if the Marshal or his lieutenant were not present, but this was a relatively junior position. Other subordinate officials included the Commander of the Vault who was in charge of stores, the Sub-Marshal and the Turcopolier who later commanded the turcopoles, and by 1248 was probably a brother-sergeant. In 1303 the office of Turcopolier was raised to the rank of a *conventual bailli* although its holder was still subordinate to the Marshal.

The **Castellans** or commanders of the Order's most important castles were also under the Marshal's authority. Some of the smaller castles did not have castellans, and some may not have been permanently garrisoned. The castellans of major Middle Eastern castles achieved the status of capitular baillis and in 1304, after all the Syrian castles had

The front and back of the 12th-century Great Seal of the Hospitaller Convent. On the back, a sick man lies on a bed beneath a lamp symbolising both the medical functions of the Order.

fallen to the Mamluks, no brother could become a castellan unless he had served in the Order for at least five years. The **Admiral** was one of the last military officials to be created, in around 1300. He was in command of all galleys and armed ships smaller than a galley, as well as of men-at-arms and sailors aboard such vessels.

A huge, widely spread and wealthy organisation like the Hospitallers naturally needed a large number of skilled civilian or non-military officials. They included the *drapier* who was in charge of clothing allocations from the *parmentarie* which seems to have been a tailoring department as well as a clothing store, where the *drapier* was assisted by a brother of the parmentarie. The latter's duties included sealing up the goods of deceased brothers. The Treasurer controlled the Treasury, while the Hospitaller was responsible for the sick, and the Conventual Prior was the Order's most senior ecclesiastical official. Other specialist officials such as the Master Crossbowman and Master Sergeant were not brothers of the Order.

Hospitaller records make the question of numbers of men – brothers and non-brothers – slightly clearer than is normal with medieval armies. Around 1169, for example, the Hospitaller Master Gilbert d'Assailly promised to supply 500 knights and 500 turcopoles for the forthcoming invasion of Egypt, but not all of them would have been brethren. Nor were the estimated 2,000 men whom the Hospitallers were said to have at the siege of Dumyat during the Fifth Crusade. In fact it seems that the Hospitallers normally only had around 300 brethren-at-arms in the Middle East at any one time, plus non-brethren sergeants, turcopoles, support personnel, etc. At the battle of La Forbie the Hospitallers lost 325 brothers-in-arms and around 200 turcopoles with only 26 Hospitallers escaping. This must have virtually wiped out the brothers-at-arms then stationed in the Middle East, but just over 20 years later the Master, Hugh Revel implied that there were once some 300 brothers in Syria. But by 1301, following the fall of Acre, the Hospitallers based at Limassol in Cyprus numbered a mere 70 brother-knights and 10 brother-sergeants. Although there were more Hospitallers elsewhere, they tended to be spread over a very wide area, even in frontier regions such as the Iberian peninsula and Hungary.

The numbers of Hospitaller brothers stationed in any particular garrison did not, of course, represent its whole military strength, with the numbers of mercenaries and other personnel normally far greater.

In 1212 the garrisons of the great castles of Krak des Chevaliers and Marqab housed 2,000 and 1,000 troops respectively, but according to a letter to the Pope in 1255 the Hospitallers only planned to have 60 cavalry in Krak. When the Hospitaller-held town of Arsuf fell to the Mamluks in 1265, 1,000 men were killed or captured, but only 80 of them were Hospitaller brethren. Nevertheless, wherever they were stationed Hospitaller brothers-in-arms formed an elite.

The territory held by the Hospitallers in the Crusader States was not particularly extensive, but it tended to be compact, well defended and fertile. The Order used their estates and other economic assets to support their defence of the Holy Land, not only by growing food, but by raising money through the export of olive oil and cane sugar. Here a Hospitaller *castellan* or *bailli* normally dealt with the peasantry through their *ra'is* or headman who might be in charge of several *casalia*, or villages. In addition to agricultural land and castles, the Hospitallers acquired decaying or defunct religious foundations, including a venerable monastery on Mount Tabor in Galilee. They also acquired urban properties such as residential houses, bakeries, mills, inns and markets, all of which had to be administered by, or on behalf of, the Hospitallers. Like other major landowners in the Crusader States, the Hospitallers owned many Muslim slaves, some captured in war, some given as the Order's share of booty, others purchased on the open market.

Communications between the Middle East and Western Europe by sea were the life-blood of the Crusader States once the overland route had been severed in the mid-12th century. But with their wide-ranging network of subordinate houses, efficient personnel and already considerable wealth, the Hospitallers were able to send men and money to the Middle East with relative ease. For example, their priories or provinces in Central and Eastern Europe were linked to the Middle East

The Hospitallers recruited many brothers and sergeants from German-speaking lands and their arms and armour are reflected in simple provincial art as well as in great German cathedrals. (In situ tympanum of Church of St Michael, Altenstadt, Germany; author's photograph)

The massive Hospitaller castle of Marqab still dominates the port-city of Banyas. Its western ramparts now look down on a strategic oil refinery. (Author's photograph)

via the River Danube, the Balkans and the Byzantine capital of Constantinople where there was even a Hospitaller *domus* (house) and a *prior* in the 1180s. With the decline of Byzantine authority in the Balkans this route became too dangerous and was replaced by overland routes to Venice and thence by sea to Syria. Men, matériel and money from priories further west seem to have been channelled through Marseilles. Even so the increasing cost of warfare, and particularly the maintenance of heavily armoured cavalry, meant that the Hospitallers became seriously short of money in the late 13th century. The Order's headquarters in the Middle East often complained that it was not receiving sufficient funds from the western priories, although they normally sent a third or more of their income east.

The growing military and economic power of the Hospitallers was one reason why the Church favoured strengthening the Order in the 12th century, and in 1154 the Pope permitted them to have their own priests who were under the same discipline as brother-knights. Those in the Middle East were under the **Conventual Prior** at the Order's headquarters, while those in Europe were subject to the regional priors.

MOTIVATION AND MORALE

The primary motivation for the men and women who joined the Order of the Hospital of St John was, of course, religious. By the time of the Crusades, the concept of holy war had been accepted by most Western European Christians. According to religious scholars, taking part in a holy war was 'commanded by God', whereas taking part in a 'just war' was merely 'allowed by God'. But the idea that men who died on crusade were martyrs seems to have been new. The recently emerged class of knights faced moral problems in their everyday role as a warrior elite

19

A – Front of the lead seal of the master, Father Roger de Moulins, showing him at prayer.
B – Back of the lead seal of Father Roger de Moulins who was killed in 1187.
C – Front and back of the Great Seal of the Master, Father Nicholas Lorgne, dating from around 1282.
D – Wax Seal of the Master, Father Hugues Revel, dating from around 1268.

which owed obedience to a secular lord. It was all very well for 12th century theologians like Stephen of Muret to suggest that while a knight could not refuse his feudal obedience, he could absolve himself by telling God that he wanted only to be a Christian knight and that he would 'seek after that which is good on every occasion as much as I can'. Joining one of the Military Orders offered a solution. According to the mid-12th century lawyer Master Rolandus, 'To kill evil persons for purposes of correction and justice is actually to minister unto God.' In other words, such violence was a form of Christian charity as summed up by the 13th century historian and Bishop of Acre, Jacques de Vitry: 'The brothers of a Military Order have been assigned the task of defending the Church of Christ against those who are not Christians, namely the Saracens in Syria, the Moors in Spain, and the pagans in Prussia, Livonia and Cumania, but also at the command of their superiors against schismatics in Greece and against heretics wherever they exist in the Universal Church.'

The religious enthusiasm of the Hospitallers, like other crusaders, was supported by the use of sacred relics such as fragments of the True Cross which accompanied armies of the Crusader States on several campaigns. A beautiful crystal reliquary in the form of a bishop's mitre set in a gilded bronze frame and containing tiny relics of the True Cross, the apostles and various saints was in fact buried in the former Hospitaller conventual church in Jerusalem. It was found by workmen near the old high altar in 1893. Brother-knights also retained the ethos and many of the attitudes of ordinary knights for whom it remained true that: 'the hermit in his cell, the monk in his cloister, the knight in his lord's household, all belonged to their distinct militia but for each the struggle could be hard and long'. Many must also have had that love of campaigning which was summed up by the southern French poet Pierre de Bergerac in the early 13th century: 'I like to hear the slap of the hauberk against the saddle-bow ... and hear the tinkling and jingling of the harness, then I rush forth and see pourpoints and gambesons, thrown on top of armour, the rustling of the pennons lifts my spirits.'

Despite its religious motivation, the Order's relations with the Papacy were not always entirely obedient, particularly when various popes wanted them to interfere in the internal affairs of the Crusader States during the 13th century. Some papal criticism of the Hospitallers may in reality have been attempts to put moral pressure on the Order as when, in March 1238, Pope Gregory IX wrote that he had heard that Hospitaller brethren kept harlots in their villages, owned private property and were even suspected of heresy. The Hospitallers were even more reluctant to get involved in European wars, and the popes knew that they would be accused of diverting the Military Order's resources if they pushed the Orders to do so. As far at the Hospitallers themselves were concerned, they came to see themselves and the rival Templars as the primary Christian military power in the Holy Land and were even reluctant to get sidetracked into the affairs of the Crusader States in Greece.

Although the Hospitallers may have become recognised experts on Middle Eastern affairs, they never bridged the cultural gap with Orthodox Christians and never fully accepted that the survival of the Crusader States depended on co-existence with Islam. In fact, the supposed toleration of Muslims by the Military Orders merely reflected the pragmatic attitudes of those who actually lived on the religious-cultural frontier. The Rule of the Templars even permitted military service in the armies of the Seljuks of Rum (Anatolia), but Hospitaller rules on this matter are unfortunately unknown.

From the other side of the frontier, the dedication of the Hospitallers is clear in many Arabic sources. The death of the Hospitaller castellan of Krak des Chevaliers in 1170 was a cause for widespread celebration among Muslims, for example. As Ibn al-Athir wrote, he had been 'a man who, through his bravery, occupied an eminent position and who was like a bone stuck in the throat of the Muslims'. According to al-Athir, Saladin executed captured Hospitallers and Templars after the battle of Hattin 'because of the violent hatred they bore against the Muslims and because of their bravery'. Al-Harawi advised Saladin's successor that he 'should beware of the warrior monks ... for he cannot achieve his goals through them, for they have great fervour in religion, paying no attention to the things of this world. He cannot prevent them from interfering in political affairs. I have investigated them extensively and have found nothing which contradicts this.' Almost a century later Abu'l-Fida celebrated the capture of the great Hospitaller castle of Marqab: 'In this memorable day were revenged the evils caused by the house of the Hospitallers and the brightness of day replaced the shadows.'

The discipline of the Hospitallers was recognised by friend and foe alike. On the other hand, a special decree issued in 1283, stating that no Hospitaller castle could surrender without first informing the Master, suggests that such an event had already happened. A few men left the Order, though they were strongly condemned for doing so. There was also friction between brother-knights and brother-sergeants who regarded the former as arrogant, while in the 13th century the status of brothers-in-service steadily declined. Christian prisoners-of-war who converted to Islam and fought against their previous comrades soon became a feature of crusading warfare, but very few of them had been members of the Military Orders and none are recorded from the Hospitallers.

A reliquary from the Church of Mar Hanna, formerly the Conventual Church of the Hospitallers, which was found in 1893 by workmen digging near the High Altar. It was probably buried in the troubled years 1242 or 1244. (Treasury of the Greek Patriarchate of the Church of Holy Sepulchre, Jerusalem)

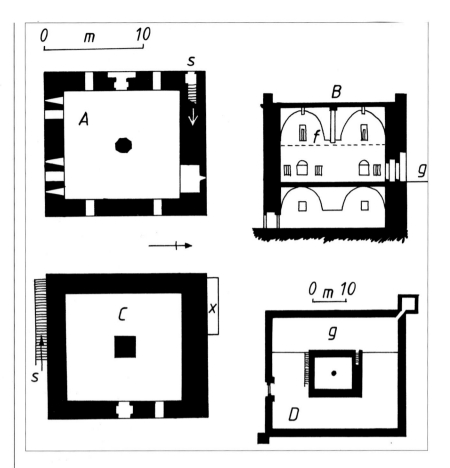

The Qala'at Yahmur on the Syrian coast (after H. Kennedy). A – first floor. B – section. C – ground floor. D – the tower and fortified compound; f – originally a wooden floor; g – terrace on west side of compound; s – stairs; x – buttress against north wall.

It is also clear that the execution of captured brothers-in-arms by the Muslims was not a general practice, and by the mid-13th century a system of prisoner exchange had developed. During the final years of the Crusader States, large numbers of Hospitallers fell into Mamluk hands and those brethren who did become prisoners-of-war could expect to languish in bad conditions or to be worked hard on construction projects for many years. One English Hospitaller, Roger of Stanegrave, was still in Mamluk hands in 1318 and was still seeking a huge ransom of 12,000 gold florins from his friends and family.

Among the regular clergy, the Military Orders were regarded as inferior because they shed blood and were not always able to fulfil every religious vigil. In return, the Hospitallers were concerned to maintain their good reputation and used remarkably sophisticated propaganda to do so. Brothers who travelled abroad were urged to behave well, scandals were kept secret from the outside world and the Order soon had permanent representatives at the papal Curia in Rome as well as at the main secular courts. The Hospitaller headquarters also sent regular reports back to Europe. Though normally addressed to a specific individual, they were clearly intended to be made public. Visible forms of 'image making' devices such as commemorative carvings, wall-paintings and round churches which symbolised the great Church of the Holy Sepulchre in Jerusalem served the same purpose. Seals were particularly useful as they were attached to documents sent throughout Christendom, and the reverse of Hospitaller seals usually showed a man lying on a mattress or bier. He represented a sick pilgrim being cared for in one of the Order's hospitals. As enthusiasm for the crusade declined, patronage was harder to find and might only be offered in return for expensive religious duties such as maintaining chantry priests who sang regular masses for the departed benefactor.

Among ordinary people, however, the Military Orders were often seen as the best part of the Church by the late 13th century, and despite scepticism the Hospitallers still enjoyed widespread support amongst European rulers. In 1274 Emperor Rudolf of Habsburg confirmed their rights and privileges in the German Empire, saying of the brethren: 'Spurning worldly conflict, they fearlessly march against the forces of the pagan pestilence, staining the standards of Christian victory and the banners of their own knighthood in the blood of the glorious martyr, they fight valiantly against the barbarian nations and they do not fear to give themselves up to a worthy death.'

The Order associated itself with popular saints and had its first two Masters portrayed as 'blessed'. Both Hospitallers and Templars wanted to be seen as 'ancient' rather than 'modern' creations. Hence the Hospitallers claimed that they had existed in the time of the Apostles, having been founded in Jerusalem at the time of the Roman Emperor Augustus. Other stories pushed the Order ever further back in history, maintaining that the Jewish hero Judas Maccabaeus was a patron of the Hospital in Jerusalem, that John the Baptist's parents had worked there, that Christ himself had paid a visit, that Christ first appeared there after his Resurrection and that St Stephen the first martyr had been a Master of this ancient hospital.

Competition between the two Military Orders became fierce following the fall of the Crusader States and the leading hero in most widely read accounts of the fall of Acre was Brother Matthew of Claremont, the marshal of the Hospitallers. 'Rushing through the midst of the troops like a raging man ... he crossed through St Anthony's Gate beyond the whole army. By his blows he threw down many of the infidels dying to the ground. For they fled from him like sheep, whither they knew not, flee before the wolf.' Matthew supposedly rode on into the middle of the city where, his horse exhausted, he made a final stand until struck down by the enemy's spears. The disasters of 1291 clearly demoralised the Order of the Hospital of St John and when even the little off-shore island of Ruad fell, both the Hospitallers and the Templars were in danger of losing their whole reason for existence. A new purpose had to be found and this would take many years of soul-searching.

COSTUME, WEAPONS AND HARNESS

Wearing colourful, expensive clothes and the use of decorated military equipment and horse-harness was very much part of the knightly way of life, but when a man entered one of the Military Orders all this changed. The Rule of the Hospitallers was emphatic on such matters, but it proved difficult to ensure that dress, harness or equipment regulations were always followed. Hospitaller *statutes* or the rulings by the Chapters constantly prohibited various forms of decorated equipment, and eventually the regulations themselves were relaxed. Some statutes shed an interesting light on how individual brethren behaved: in 1262 one forbade the wearing of *espaliers d'armes* (mail or padded shoulder defences) or *chausses* (mail leg protections) at prayers. Another dated 4 August 1278 insisting that no armour be worn within the precincts of the Hospitaller convent during the elections of a new Master hints at previous attempts at intimidation by armed men.

No Hospitaller brother-in-arms was allowed more than the regulation amount of military equipment unless given special permission. This may simply have reflected the limited amount of kit available and shortages could have accounted for the Hospitallers' recycling of arms, armour, horse-harness and even clothing, all of which reverted to the Order on a brother's death. Since the Master, Grand Commander, Marshal, Hospitaller, Informarian, Drapier, Treasurer and Con-ventual Prior all had claims on such material there could be confusion so the issue was carefully regulated.

Mid-13th century Hospitaller *usances* (customs) show that the matériel was divided into distinct sections. Horses and related equipment went to the Marshal, as did arms and armour, bedding went to the Drapier as did most clothing and unused cloth. Table and kitchen items, books, liturgical and other miscellaneous objects held by capitular bailiffs and those of the master's companions went to the Master. Those of other brethren-at-arms went to the Marshal, but those of regular bailiffs and all brethren-in-office went to the Grand Commander. Any money probably went to the treasury.

The chapel in the Hospitaller castle of Marqab is a simple, almost stark structure with no carved decoration. (Author's photograph)

A – The so-called Cloister in the massive Hospitaller castle of Krak des Chevaliers runs along one side of the main courtyard. Behind it is the Chapter House or council chamber. (Author's photograph)
B – One of the carved capitals in the Cloister at Krak des Chevaliers. (Author's photograph)

LEFT A very damaged section of a 13th century wall-painting from a chapel in Beirut, showing a 'donor figure' adoring the Virgin and Child. (Formerly in the National Museum, Beirut, present whereabouts unknown; E. Cruikshank-Dodd photograph)

According to a *statute* of 1288, armour was also handed back when a brother left the Middle East. It was available to other brothers-in-arms who might want to make an exchange for what they already had. Crossbows were a special case, since these had to be placed in the treasury. Later *usances* were more detailed, specifying that Turkish carpets, saddles, javelins, *bardings* (horse coverings), *gonfanons* (flags), *pennoncelles* (small pennons), chargers (war horses), hacks (riding horses), mules, Turkish weapons, axes, all forms of armour and harness for animals, *arcs de bodoc* (pellet bows), table knives, crossbows, all forms of armour (for men), swords, lances, *coreaus de fetur* (leather cuirasses), *playines* (plate armour), mail hauberks, *gipelles* (quilted soft armours), *soubre seignals* (perhaps surcoats), *chapels de fer* (brimmed helmets) and *bascinets* (close fitting helmets) of dead brothers went to the Marshal.

Uniform

The habit or costume of the Hospitallers was a genuine uniform, but was more suited to the life of a monk. The standard black *cappae* were relatively tight fitting monastic robes which brothers-in-arms had to wear over their armour. It was clearly not suited to the violent movement of close combat, yet it was not until 1248 that Pope Innocent IV allowed the brothers-in-arms to 'wear wide surcoats, bearing upon the breast the sign of the Cross', although only in 'dangerous areas'. Crosses were sewn on the breasts of the capes and mantles, but could apparently be removed when travelling in non-Christian countries. In the late 13th and early 14th centuries the brothers' mantle folded entirely

25

Two Latin priests, monks or perhaps members of a Military Order, on a wall-painting of the Dormition of the Virgin made around 1248 in the Lebanese village of Ma'ad. (In situ Church of St Sharbel, Ma'ad, Lebanon; E. Cruikshank-Dodd photo)

around the body and opened in front where it could be closed by buttons of the same cloth. On the front was a cross, 7–10 cm wide in the characteristic eight-pointed Hospitaller form first seen in the early 13th century. The conventual shoes worn on most occasions are not really understood, but were presumably simple.

Coloured cloth, velvet and the skins of wild animals were strictly prohibited, yet the normal clothing issue seemed lavish by the standards of the time. It consisted of three shirts, three pairs breeches, one *cotta* or tunic, one monastic habit, one *garnache* (coat and hood), two mantles or cloaks one of which was lined with fur, one pair linen hose and one of wool, three bed-sheets and a sack in which to keep them. The reforms of 1295 mentioned a yearly issue of two suits consisting of a tunic and undertunic, hooded coat, and mantle one of which was lined with fur. These included the livery or heavier ceremonial robes and the thinner 'robes of pittance' used in summer. *Hargans* (long coats) and *cotes hardies* (short coats) were originally forbidden, but long coats were acceptable by 1300 when they had to bear the cross of the order. Short coats with points (laces to which the hose and other garments could be attached) were, however, still unacceptable. A further decree of 1305 stated that the mantle, robes, *rondel* (probably a type of scarf) and long coat must all be black.

On his head a brother wore a white coif which at first had to be of double thickness, and later became 'simple'. Except during certain church services, the coif was covered by a large skull cap which had to touch the wearer's ears on both sides. In the 1280s a *usance* repeated that a brother might not remove his *biretta* or hat even if he was feeling hot, unless there was a good reason. A brother could also wear a brimmed hat, white turban or *oreillet* (item covering the ears) in the fierce Middle Eastern sun. In 1262 another *statute* stated that on a military expedition no brother could wear a turban which was anything other than white, which was embroidered or which dangled down to his waist.

In the first Hospitaller Rule, brothers were not allowed *planeaus* (sandals) or *galoches* (large overshoes as worn in the Islamic world) but only wore *soliers* or ordinary shoes. From the late 12th century a Hospitaller brother was permitted boots during the night, and a complex set of regulations developed which allowed him to keep his boots on at other times. A reaction may have set in at Acre in 1270 when a *statute* stated that all *estiveaus* or boots, perhaps of the soft Middle Eastern variety, were prohibited except when a man was armed. Yet the problem of footwear continued, and in late 13th century Cyprus, pointed boots and fashionable *chauses avantpiés* (hose incorporating pointed toes) were prohibited. The cost of such clothing was clearly very high, and from the mid-13th century many brothers were issued a set amount of money to buy their own clothes. Each brother was also given what could be called pocket-money, but the vain were said to have wasted this on more fashionable clothes and even jewellery.

In 1259 Pope Alexander IV granted a distinctive costume to the brother-knights of the Hospitallers, there previously having been no difference between the dress of knights and sergeants: 'The knights who are brethren in your Order shall wear black mantles in order that they may be distinguished from the other brethren of the said Order [who presumably wore dark brown]. In war, however, and in battle they shall wear jupons and other military surcoats which shall be of a red colour, having sewn upon them a white cross exactly as upon your standard.' The new rule was revoked after nineteen years, perhaps having had a bad effect on morale within the Order, and all brethren-in-arms soon wore a scarlet surcoat in battle.

Arms

The *guarnement* or arms and armour used by Hospitaller brothers-in-arms was the same as that of other knights and sergeants, except for its lack of decoration. During the 12th century it usually consisted of a shield, surcoat, sword, sometimes a *coutel* or dagger, a mail hauberk, *afeutreüre* which may have been an early form of soft-armour worn beneath the *hauberk*, quilted *cuisses* for the thighs, sometimes mail *chauses*, a helmet, and a long cavalry lance or shorter infantry spear. The mace was, however, still regarded as an Islamic weapon or one used by non-noble infantry. The quilted *aketon*, *gambais* and *gambeson* were worn beneath, or sometimes over, other armour in the 13th century, but in the Middle East knights, including members of the Military Orders, sometimes wore quilted armour without the heavier mail hauberk, particularly in summer, when scouting or harassing the enemy as light cavalry.

There is little evidence of iron equipment being made in the Crusader States, and almost all the arms and armour used by the Hospitallers was imported from Europe. Although it was very expensive there were big variations in cost between different items. In late 12th to mid-13th century Genoa, for example, a mail hauberk was approximately five times as expensive as a separate mail coif, while a cuirass and a *panceria* (light mail armour) were less than half that of a hauberk. Comparable information from Venice indicates that a helmet cost 30 denarii, a sword from 45 to 50 denarii, a knife or dagger 20 denarii, and even a crossbow arrow cost 1 denarius. In 1262 it cost 2,000 silver deniers de Tours to fully equip a Hospitaller knight; in 1303

A head from a shattered late 13th century English effigy shows a ventail laced to the left side of the head, a narrow lace to secure the mail coif and a broader band which probably supported a helmet. (In situ church, Farnborough, Warwickshire, England; author's photograph)

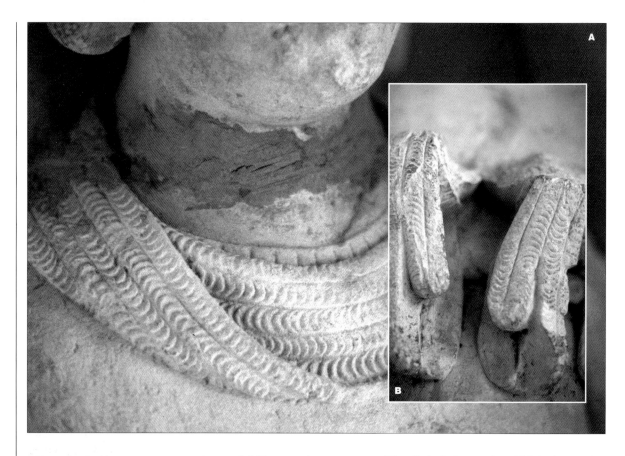

A

B

Unfortunately most French effigies were destroyed in the Revolution, but one 13th century example came from Ouville l'Abbaye. A: the neck of the effigy shows an unlined mail coif, a hauberk and what is probably the neck of an aketon or gambeson. (Musée des Antiquités, Rouen, France; author's photograph) B: the damaged wrists of this effigy show the quilted cuffs of the same aketon or gambeson. (Musée des Antiquités, Rouen, France; author's photograph)

it cost 1,500 to equip a sergeant. The little information which does refer to arms manufacture in the Crusader States indicates that shields were made in Jerusalem and crossbows in Acre. A chronic shortage of military equipment is also indicated by the Hospitallers' overriding concern that weaponry move only from Europe to the Crusader States. Brothers going back to Europe were issued with the barest minimum, whereas senior officials coming from Europe normally brought what was described as a 'passage of armour'. Ordinary brethren were expected to bring full military kit and in 1293 the Master Jean de Villiers ruled that brothers returning from the West must also bring three 'beasts' – horses and pack animals.

As far as weapons were concerned, the cavalry lance remained the most important. It was normally about 3 metres long with a shaft, often of spruce. An object called a *hantier* appears in some early 13th century sources, and this may have been a support for the butt of the lance while it was being carried vertically. The sword was the most prestigious weapon, but was of secondary importance in a cavalry charge, Most surviving examples weigh from 1–1.5 kg. Daggers were widely used in the Islamic world, but in 12th century Europe seem to have been despised by the knightly elite. It may therefore be significant that some of the earliest references to a *misericorde* or *coutel* dagger in medieval Western literature are associated with the crusades or Military Orders. Maces were also considered 'Saracenic' until the 13th century, while axes, *guisarmes d'acier* (long-hafted axe) and *faussars affilés* (long bladed infantry weapon) were all used by Christian infantry.

Hospitaller statutes stated that brothers-in-arms should tie their armour in a bundle and place it behind their saddle while on campaign, but should always wear helmets and leg armour in hostile territory. Less is known about the armour itself, although the Hospitallers placed great emphasis on the possession of 'suitable' equipment. Some of it is likely to have reflected oriental or Islamic influence, particularly the use of hardened leather defences in the 13th and 14th centuries, and, of course, in a fabric covered form of mail hauberk, known in the late 12th century Crusader States as the *auberc jaserant*. This was merely the Arab-Islamic *khazaghand*.

Other less common forms of body armour included leather armour called *coirasses* in the Iberian peninsinula and *cuiries* in France – the coat-of-plates which first appeared in the second half of the 13th century; the *panceriam* which sometimes had only one integral mitten. The *manicle de fer* or integral mail mitten at the end of the long sleeves of a mail hauberk first appeared in the late 12th century. Additional protections for the legs developed earlier than those for the arms. An early 13th century section of the *Old French Crusade Cycle* mentions *genellières* 'hanging like window coverings', which may have been an early form of knee defence.

The First Crusade in the earliest surviving manuscript from the Crusader States. It shows an early form of flat-topped great helm. (*Histoire Universelle*, Vatican Library, M.S.Pal.Lat. 1963, f, 31v, Rome)

Helmets were kept in place by laces or chin-straps, which fastened over the ventail or mail flap protecting the throat and chin. The increasing threat from crossbows and from composite bows in the Middle East led to greater protection for a warrior's face. At first this took the form of a broader nasal but gradually rigid visors were attached to helmets of various shapes. A section of the *Old French Crusade Cycle*, called *Le Chevalier au Cigne*, dating from the late 12th or early 13th century provides an early description of such a helmet which included a *maistre* or bowl, *candelabres* which may have been a strengthening frame or rim, a *fenestral* which seems to have been the visor itself, a traditional nasal to which the visor might have been attached, a *mentonal* or chin-strap, and *uellière* or eye-slits. Pictorial evidence shows that the next form of separate, small and hemispherical *cervellière* helmet was sometimes worn beneath a mail coif but as it increased in size with extensions to protect the sides and back of the head, it was worn over a coif. The coif itself was occasionally described as *fort et turcoise* which possibly meant having its own quilted lining. By the late 12th century the term *clavain* appeared, but it is unclear whether this was regarded as the neck part of the coif or was, more likely, the reinforced neck part of a hauberk which might otherwise lack an integral coif.

An English effigy dating from the late 13th century shows a mail coif worn over a flat-topped arming cap which would have supported a great helm. (In situ church Abbey Dore, Herefordshire, England; author's photograph)

European and thus also Hospitaller shields were almost invariably of wood and were usually covered in leather, but their size, shape and thickness changed considerably from the 12th to 13th centuries. One of few specialised forms was the very large *talevas* used by men on foot which might better be called a mantlet since it could be rested on the ground.

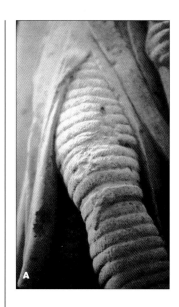

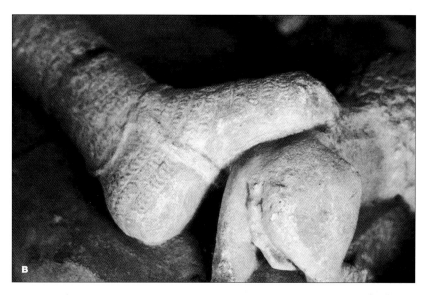

A: Detail of the knee of an effigy showing a narrow buckled lace beneath the knee which stopped the mail chausses from flapping about. B: Detail of the foot of an effigy showing that the mail did not go beneath the foot where there is a leather sole. (In situ church, Tickenham, Somerset, England; author's photographs)

The horse harness used by Hospitallers was undecorated, but the basic elements were the same as those of ordinary knights. In the late 12th century the preparation of a war-horse for battle involved putting on and checking the *caignle, sorcaingles* and *poitral* which were the three main straps securing the saddle. War saddles themselves had *arcons* or extensions of the raised cantle or rear of the saddle which went around the lower part of the rider's hips. Under the saddle saddle-cloths rather than all-enveloping caparisons or bards. Another term for these may have been *senbues*. The seat or cushion of the saddle may have been called a *panel*. A legal decision reached by the Hospitaller headquarters in 1303 made a clear distinction between 'Turkish saddles', ordinary riding saddles and war-saddles. The regulation also stated that war-saddles must not be used by warriors of Syrian origin because they were turcopoles rather than knights. Horse-armour had been widely used in the Islamic world since the 8th century, but did not appear in Western Europe until the late 12th century, and then clearly as a result of Islamic influence. Such protections remained very expensive, even for the Military Orders, and it seems that armoured horses remained very rare within the Crusader States.

TRAINING, STRATEGY AND TACTICS

Little is known about military training within the Military Orders, despite the fact that young novices must have entered with very limited military skills. Their initial training seems to have been informal and took about a year, being based upon practical texts in French rather than translations of archaic Latin texts. On the other hand most Hospitaller brethren-at-arms were trained soldiers before they joined the Order. It was popularly said in 12th century Western Europe that, 'You can make a horseman of a lad at puberty, but after that never. He who stays at school until the age of twelve is fit only to be a priest.' But there was no prejudice against literacy in the knightly class, as Abbot Philip de Bonne-Esperance wrote to Count Philip of Flanders around 1168: 'for many, chivalry does not preclude learning, nor does knowledge of letters in a moral cause preclude chivalry'. It is also worth noting that in the German prose version of the *Romance of Lancelot*, the hero's guardian sent him directly from his nurses to a monk who taught Lancelot to read and write.

From the age of 12 the education of young warriors focused on riding, discipline, the use of lance and shield, and an ability to evade enemy blows. During the 12th century the tournament and jousting ceased to be a genuine form of military exercise and became a sport. Perhaps for this reason Hospitaller regulations only permitted limited practice jousts in the presence of the Master. Hunting anything other than lions, which were still a hazard in the Middle East, was also banned, although by the 13th century unauthorised hunting was only seen as a minor offence. Crossbows could only be used against targets – in other words in military training – and there are plenty of references to knights using them.

The *couched* lance, firmly tucked beneath a cavalryman's arm and used in a close-packed *conrois* of horsemen, demanded considerable discipline and unit cohesion. It also entailed the proper use of a shield, as the *Song of Roland* said: 'Shields on their necks and with their lances well ordered.' Such group training had the added advantage of developing strong comradeship. The couched lance not only added weight, and thus penetration to a thrust, but enabled a successful cavalryman to topple a foe from his saddle or even overthrow both man and horse, as the *Song of Roland* again eloquently put it: 'The girths are burst, the saddles swivel round.'

The little evidence which survives from the medieval period indicates that swordsmanship was firmly associated with the use of the shield. Available literary and pictorial sources also have interesting similarities with training manuals from Byzantine and Islamic literature. Unlike the gentlemanly duelling of later centuries, medieval fencing relied on a

The Hospitaller castle at Belvoir in Palestine. A: plan of castle. B: reconstruction of castle.

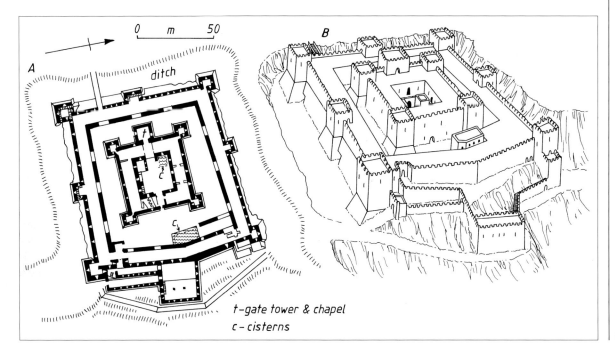

t-gate tower & chapel
c - cisterns

heavy blade to cope with the greater variety of helmets, armour and opposing weapons. Thrusts were usually aimed at the opponent's face, cuts were directed against legs and feet, while defensive parries used both sword and shield. Thrusts were also considered more effective than cuts.

Crusading warfare was significantly more dangerous than knightly combat in Western Europe, and members of Military Orders would have expected to suffer higher casualties, particularly numerous facial injuries from archery. The Hospitallers' leading military role also meant that they lost a great many horses. Nevertheless, the idea that the heavily armoured knights dominated the battlefield is a myth, even within Europe. Cavalry almost invariably needed the support of good infantry, but men on horseback, whether they were heavily armoured, lighter cavalry, or mounted infantry did predominate in the raiding warfare which played a major role in the Crusader States.

Where the Military Orders were concerned a campaign would begin with the brothers mustering in their quarters with horses, pack animals and livestock to provide food on the hoof. At this stage they were under the command of the Marshal, but would often be transferred to the Gonfanonier as a raid set out. When larger armies were on the move, the Hospitallers and Templars often provided van and rearguards, the Hospitallers being in the rearguard at the battle of Arsuf during the Third Crusade.

The Rule of the Templars provides detailed information which is lacking for the Hospitallers, but they are likely to have been very similar.

Knight and sergeant uniforms
1: Brother-in-arms, c.1160
2: Brother sergeant-at-arms, c.1250
3: Brother knight-at-arms, c.1275
4: Brother knight-at-arms, c.1305

A

B Treating wounded in the hospital, early 12th century

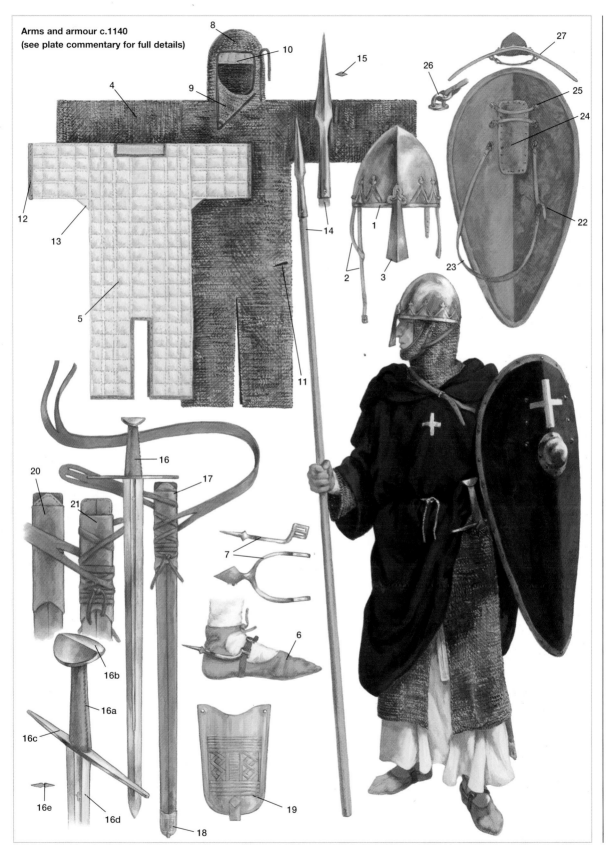

Arms and armour c.1140
(see plate commentary for full details)

c

Defending pilgrims c.1150

D

Clothing allocation according to the Hospitaller statute of 1206 (see plate commentary for full details)

Caravan raid c.1250

F

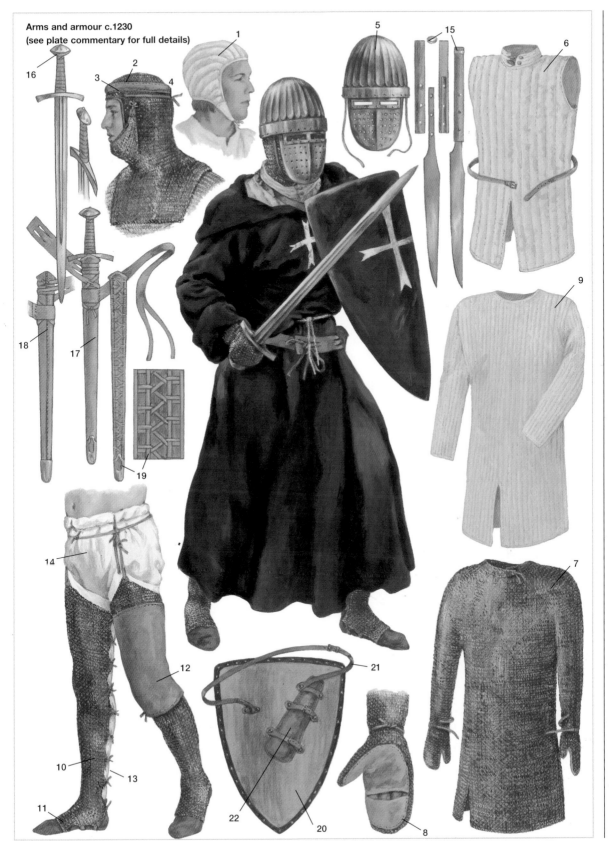

Arms and armour c.1230
(see plate commentary for full details)

G

A meeting of the Chapter c.1270

The banner of the Order of the Hospital of St John
and the coats of arms of its masters to 1306
(see plate commentary for full details)

The fall of Acre, 1291

These simple late-12th or early-13th century wall-paintings show knightly opponents using lances and then fighting with swords. (In situ, Church of All Saints, Claverley, Shropshire, England; author's photographs)

When a Templar force was preparing to march, for example, the brother-knights assembled ahead with the squires following with the baggage. Once they were ready to move, the squires rode ahead with the knights' weapons and spare horses. Secular sources indicate that the raising of banners was taken as a signal for a force to move. Hospitaller statutes indicate they were usually accompanied by priests, probably from the Order itself, that there should be no individual looting and that all booty was assembled collectively. In hostile territory brother-knights rode with their shields, and when near to the enemy they put on helmets. In friendly territory, however, the shields were carried by squires or servants. Again, Templar sources are more detailed. For example if a man wanted to change position on the march he did so downwind from the main body, so that he did not kick dust into their eyes. In peacetime the men could water their horses at streams, but in enemy country they could only do so when the Gonfanonier signalled a halt. If an alarm sounded, those closest should mount their horses, take up their weapons and await orders while those further away should muster around the Master.

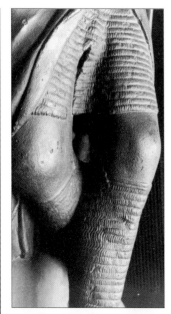

Fortunately plaster casts were made of the superb effigies in London's Temple Church before they were damaged in the Second World War. TOP: the effigy of William Marshal the Younger shows chausses secured by a narrow knotted lace or thong. BOTTOM: the sword, scabbard and sword-belt on the effigy of Gilbert Marshal. (Victoria and Albert Museum, London, England; author's photograph)

Similarly if an encampment was attacked, those nearest the threat hurried to repel the enemy, while the others mustered in the chapel-tent for orders. On campaign the Templars and presumably the Hospitallers erected their tents around such a chapel-tent. All equipment was put inside their tents, and servants were sent to forage for firewood and water, although they could not go beyond earshot. Imad al-Din al-Isfahani described one skirmish between Saladin's reconnaissance units and a crusader force from Saffuriyah, adding the strange observation that as the crusaders charged 'The Templars were humming like bees, the Hospitallers bellowing like the wind.'

Large-scale training for battle did not exist during this period, but large forces did move in a co-ordinated manner, as described by the Anglo-Norman chronicler Wace: 'Those on foot led the way, in serried ranks bearing bows. The knights rode close, protecting the archers from behind. Those on horse and those on foot, just as they had begun, kept their order and the same pace, in close ranks and at a slow march, so that no-one might overtake another, nor get too close nor too far apart.' The similarity with 12th century Arab (though not Turkish) tactics is astonishing. Great discipline was required of crusader armies since their tactics normally left the initiative to their Islamic foes. Under such circumstances the steadiness of the Military Orders must have been invaluable. According to Templar sources, no man could leave his position in the ranks once an army was arrayed, unless it was to test his horse and saddle, or to help a comrade in distress. If a man wanted to speak to the master he had to go on foot and then return to his place, perhaps because riding off on horseback might cause alarm. On campaign the Military Orders certainly operated in *eschielles*, or squadrons under nominated leaders. They were smaller than a *conrois*, though the term may have referred to a tactical rather than organisational unit. Each *conrois* numbered between 20 and 40 men drawn up in two or three ranks, while several *conrois* drawn up in line formed a *bataille* or battlefield division.

It is possible that crossbowmen overcame the weapon's slow rate of fire by loosing concentrated volleys when lightly armoured Islamic horse-archers came close. It also seems clear that a substantial proportion of infantry in the Crusader States, including Hospitaller brother-sergeants, were quite heavily armoured. The renowned discipline of the Hospitallers made them less vulnerable to horse-archers than most Western European cavalry, especially when they were operating in close co-operation with disciplined infantrymen.

The structure of a crusader cavalry charge was more complex than might be thought. The Gonfanonier organised squadrons of squires with spare war-horses who could ride behind the brother-knights as they charged, while other squires with riding horses remained close to the banner. The turcopoles could also charge behind the knights in case they needed support or rescue. Brother-sergeants sometimes charged with the knights or formed a supporting rank. It was important for the horses to remain very close together, but the charge itself was probably only at a trot, perhaps spurring into a canter just before impact. An ill-considered charge might itself be hit in the flank or rear but in the mêlée or close-combat which followed a successful charge no man should leave his position even if wounded.

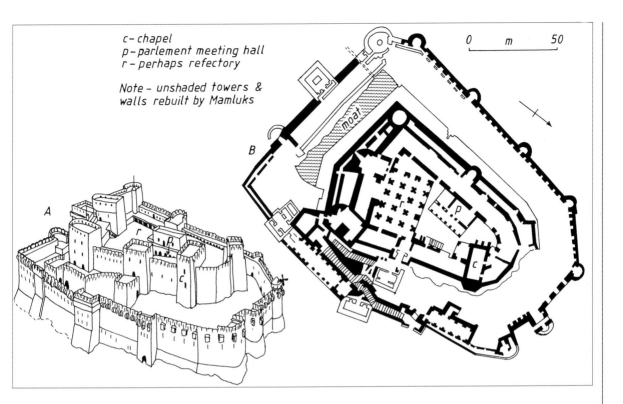

c – chapel
p – parlement meeting hall
r – perhaps refectory

Note – unshaded towers &
walls rebuilt by Mamluks

0   m   50

The Hospitaller castle at Krak des Chevaliers in Syria.
A: reconstruction of castle.
B: plan of castle.

Both Christian and Islamic sources indicate that it was difficult to knock an armoured Western knight from his saddle. Muslim soldiers were therefore trained to attack the Crusaders' horses rather than their riders. Abu Shama described the result at the battle of Hattin: 'A Frankish knight, as long as his horse was in good condition, could not be knocked down. Covered with mail from head to foot, which made him look like a block of iron, the most violent blows make no impression on him. But once his horse was killed, the knight was thrown and taken prisoner. Consequently though we counted them (Frankish prisoners) by the thousand, there were no horses amongst the spoils whereas the knights were unhurt.' Under such circumstances it was important for brethren-at-arms not to become scattered – hence the supreme importance of standards as rallying points – and some Military Orders had regulations stating how a man should rally to the banner of another Order, or indeed any Christian banner if his own fell.

Siege warfare was equally important to the Hospitallers. According to Abbot Guibert de Nogent, writing in the early 12th century, knights were assigned to wooden siege towers so that they could fight similarly well-armoured opponents defending the walls opposite them. It was, however, a dangerous position as the besieging knights were exposed to archery, crossbow fire and javelins which could pierce armour at short range. When defending a fortification, a Hospitaller garrison employed sorties as was usual, though not necessarily by knights. During Saladin's attack on the Hospitaller castle of Belvoir, for example, there was a sortie by 200 crossbowmen described as 'skilled in mountain warfare'. During the Mamluks' final siege of Acre, both the Hospitallers and the Templars made large-scale sorties against the enemy's left and right flanks, though with minimal success.

The Hospitallers had enjoyed considerable freedom of action during the 13th century, with the right to make local alliances and exploit Mongol raids, as well as internal Islamic quarrels. This was particularly true along the borders of Antioch, Tripoli and Cilician Armenia. In fact, the secular rulers of these Crusader States agreed to abide by truces arranged by the Hospitallers, whereas the Hospitallers could ignore truces negotiated by the secular rulers. In the kingdom of Jerusalem the Military Orders did not have this freedom of action, but this autonomy could lead to problems. During a crusade of 1239–41, the Muslim rulers of Damascus and Cairo were at loggerheads; the Hospitallers wanted to support Cairo but the Templars wanted to support Damascus. The Hospitallers may also have assumed the same freedom of diplomatic action elsewhere, sometimes going against papal policy as a letter from Pope Gregory IX to the Hospitallers in 1238 made clear: 'You are not ashamed to give aid against the Latins in horses and arms to Vatatses [the Byzantine Emperor John Ducas Vataces].' This was done in return for land and farms.

The question of whether or not the Crusader States should seek an alliance with the Mongol invaders of the Middle East was more serious. Eventually the Mongol invasion was rolled back by the Mamluks of Egypt, but the Hospitaller castle of Marqab was taken by the Mamluks in retaliation for the help the Hospitallers had given to their foes. An alliance between the Hospitallers and the ruling dynasty of Cilician Armenia was also influenced by the Mongol question, particularly after the Armenians became the Mongols' enthusiastic allies. It was even said that in 1281 the Prior of England and other Hospitaller brethren-in-arms fought alongside King Hethoum of Cilician Armenia and his Mongol allies against the Mamluks, though this is probably a myth.

Hospitaller castles served the same function as other Crusader fortifications. In the early days they were primarily a base for offensive

Penthesilea, Queen of the Amazons, as illustrated in a copy of William of Tyre's *Histoire Universelle*. Queen Penthesilea rides an armoured horse, but the horse armour is more Middle Eastern than European in design. (Bibliothèque Nationale, Ms. Fr. 20125, f.141v, Paris, France)

operations, although they also served as places of refuge. In the later years, these castles could not plug an invasion route, but they provided defence in depth as their garrisons could threaten an invader's communications or supply lines. Many of the most impressive Hospitaller castles were located in rugged, inaccessible areas where they were difficult to reach but this did not make them invulnerable. They may have been difficult to bombard with existing siege machines, but Islamic armies normally enjoyed a considerable superiority in infantry, and foot soldiers could harass the defenders physically and morally by repeated small assaults against different sections of wall.

The psychological aspects of medieval siege warfare have rarely been studied, but the emphasis which Military Orders such as the Hospitallers put upon communications suggests that they were fully aware of the feeling of isolation in garrisons. The Hospitallers quickly copied the Muslims' highly developed pigeon-postal system. A letter written by Jacques de Vitry in 1217 explained how they were used when Krak des Chevaliers was threatened: 'When on account of our fear of the pagans we would not dare to send messengers, we used to send pigeons carrying our letters under their wings to summon men of the city to us.' A Scottish source described how in 1266 a Hospitaller raid won considerable booty from the Mamluks: 'And the brothers of the Hospital sent to the Hospital (the headquarters in Acre) their pigeon with a letter concerning their deed.' This message was premature, however, as the raiders were ambushed on their way home.

The Master of the Hospitallers, Jean de Villiers, survived the fall of Acre in 1291 and escaped to Cyprus, although he was severely wounded. The Order's headquarters was then re-established in Cyprus but, following fears of a Mamluk naval invasion, the new Master, Guillaume de Villaret, wanted to move all the way back to Provence in southern France. He was dissuaded, however, and a new hospital was built for pilgrims at Limassol in Cyprus and the island itself was considered as a base for any future Crusades. Unfortunately Cyprus was not fertile enough and lacked sufficient good harbours; even the Hospitallers had too few properties on the island to finance the forces stationed there. For a time Cilicia seemed to offer an alternative, but it was rejected as unsuitable and too vulnerable. Transferring the Hospitaller headquarters to Byzantine territory was politically impossible – unless, of course, the Hospitallers seized some Byzantine territory for themselves. One thing was now clear. Crusading warfare against the Mamluks would henceforth be primarily naval. So the Hospitallers limited their numbers in Cyprus and concentrated on building up their fleet. In 1306 the Pope gave the Order a licence to arm its ships, which the king of Cyprus had so far refused, and that same year the Hospitaller invasion of Byzantine Rhodes began.

In another copy of the *Histoire Universelle* by William of Tyre a team of unarmoured men prepare to pull the ropes on an early form of man-powered stone-throwing mangonel. (M.E. Saltykov-Shchredrin State Library, Ms. Fr. v.IV.5, St Petersburg, Russia)

SUPPORT SERVICES

There was only minimal manufacture of military equipment in the Crusader States, so the Hospitallers brought matériel from Western Europe and were often exempt from the taxes imposed on those exporting armaments. Siege machinery was made locally, however, and Hospitaller castles often had stone-throwing mangonels in their arsenals. How the materials were purchased, and how specialist operatives were recruited remains unknown, but the Hospitallers were clearly capable of sending a substantial siege train on major expeditions.

Horses were similarly in great demand, the First Crusade having rebuilt its devastated supply from local stocks at the beginning of the 12th century. Horses were generally cheaper in southern Europe than in the Middle East. Throughout the Crusader period the cost of an ordinary warhorse was around the same as 12 head of cattle. Ordinary riding horses were cheaper still, and packhorses even more so. Recent archaeological evidence from Western Europe indicates a remarkable range in the size of horses used in the Middle Ages, from animals comparable to Shetland ponies to horses as large as 16 hands.

The Hospitallers raised some horses on their own farms, but most horses and mules still had to be shipped from Sicily to the Crusader States in great numbers during the 13th century. Brothers-in-arms of the Military Orders could not choose their own mounts, although they could request a change if they found themselves with a 'puller, stopper or thrower'. On campaign such troublesome horses were returned to the supply train. A regulation issued between 1287 and 1290 by the commander of Cyprus said that all horses had to be clipped 'in accordance with custom', but further details are not known.

The Hospitallers had only a few transport ships of their own in the 12th century. By the 1230s they were based at Marseilles where the

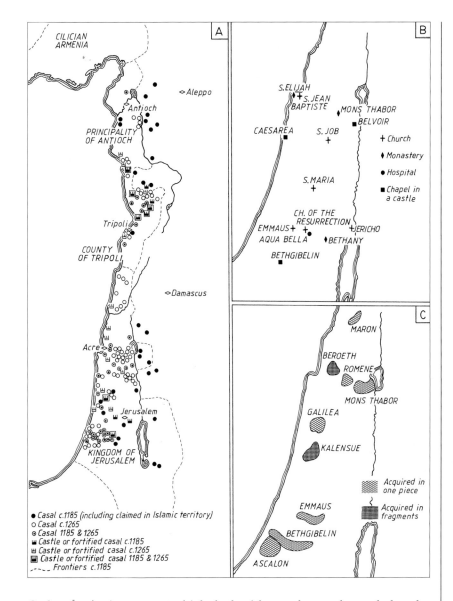

A: possessions of the Hospitallers in the Crusader States around 1185 and 1265 (after M. Balard.
B: Hospitaller religious installations in the kingdom of Jerusalem.
C: main areas of Hospitaller agricultural estates in the kingdom of Jerusalem (after M. Balard).

Map A labels: CILICIAN ARMENIA, Aleppo, Antioch, PRINCIPALITY OF ANTIOCH, Tripoli, COUNTY OF TRIPOLI, Damascus, Acre, Jerusalem, KINGDOM OF JERUSALEM

Map A legend:
● Casal c.1185 (including claimed in Islamic territory)
○ Casal c.1265
◉ Casal 1185 & 1265
▥ Castle or fortified casal c.1185
▥ Castle or fortified casal c.1265
▥ Castle or fortified casal 1185 & 1265
---- Frontiers c.1185

Map B labels: S.ELIJAH, S.JEAN BAPTISTE, MONS THABOR, BELVOIR, CAESAREA, S.JOB, S.MARIA, CH. OF THE RESURRECTION, EMMAUS, JERICHO, AQUA BELLA, BETHANY, BETHGIBELIN

Map B legend:
+ Church
◆ Monastery
● Hospital
■ Chapel in a castle

Map C labels: MARON, BEROETH, ROMENE, MONS THABOR, GALILEA, KALENSUE, EMMAUS, BETHGIBELIN, ASCALON

Map C legend:
▥ Acquired in one piece
▤ Acquired in fragments

Order also had a convent which dealt with merchants who traded to the east. The Hospitallers' Commander of Ships was probably based at Marseilles from the mid-13th century, being responsible for the construction and fitting out of vessels. His main task was to ship material east, and the ships usually made two passages each year in spring and autumn, sailing in convoy. The Commander of Ships was also responsible for feeding the brothers at sea, though a sergeant-at-arms was in charge of the actual provisions, and a commander of brothers commanded the men while at sea. He also had authority over the commander of the ship.

The numbers of people which such ships could carry sometimes seems astonishing, but the evidence is quite consistent. During the 13th century it seems to have been common for 450 pilgrims to sail aboard an ordinary transport ship; nor were the fares particularly expensive. The 1,000 troops who crowded aboard the largest transports during the Fourth Crusade might be a special case, but a quarter of

ABOVE **The extensive but undecorated chambers on the north side of the huge Hospitaller castle of Krak des Chevaliers may have been used as barracks. (Author's photograph)**

LEFT **Occasionally medieval carvings show armoured men wearing civilian hats, as was also suggested in some of the written sources. This little corbel dates from the late 13th or early 14th century and portrays a man with a mail coif plus a large hat. (In situ church, Bures, Suffolk, England; author's photograph)**

a century earlier, a Venetian transport ship squeezed almost 1,500 refugees aboard in an emergency. When Acre fell in 1291, most of those who escaped seem to have been taken by small coastal vessels to larger vessels off-shore or directly to Cyprus, and the Hospitallers played a leading role in organising this evacuation.

The Hospitallers' first attempts at naval warfare were on a small scale and in 1291, when Acre fell, some Hospitaller galleys were sent east on the Pope's direct orders. By 1300 the Hospitallers had ten galleys based in Cyprus and they joined Templar and Cypriot vessels in raiding the Egyptian and Syrian coasts. They also tried to police the trade between Italy and Mamluk Egypt, a large part of this having been declared 'illegal'

ABOVE **The eastern side of the early Hospitaller castle of Belvoir, overlooking the deep Jordan valley. A small arch near the centre of this picture was the main entrance. (Author's photograph)**

RIGHT **This early Islamic khan for merchants in Acre was incorporated into a huge complex of buildings forming the Hospitallers' hospital or hospice, headquarters and offices in the 12th and 13th centuries. (Z. Goldman photograph)**

by the Pope, but the naval power of the Hospitallers, Templars, Cypriots and papal ships remained far less than that of Genoa or Venice and the trade in strategic goods such as timber and weaponry continued.

EVERYDAY LIFE

The everyday life of the Hospitallers was governed by their Rule which was basically that of a monastic order. Outside their conventual life, however, Hospitallers had more dealings with the secular world than most monks. They not only campaigned against the enemies of the

Crusader States, but also supervised the *casalia* (farms) and other economic assets which were the Order's powerbase. This involved them in complex business transactions, banking, trade, long-distance communications and a substantial bureaucracy.

The idea that the Hospitallers lived in castles is also misleading. In the shrinking Crusader States, few lived on rural farms and more were based in flourishing coastal cities which had largely retained the Islamic or Middle Eastern character they acquired before the arrival of the First Crusade. French would have been the most common language amongst the Crusader elite, though Italian was widespread amongst the merchant middle class; Greek, Armenian and Arabic were spoken by the indigenous Christian population.

In Jerusalem the Hospitallers' conventual buildings and infirmary or hospital were south of the Holy Sepulchre. The main church had previously been Greek Orthodox and the conventual buildings clustered around it, while the huge hospital and hospices for poor pilgrims were further south. The Hospitallers also had a large house in Acre to which a hospital was added by 1172. Following the loss of Jerusalem in 1187 and the transfer of the Order's headquarters to Acre, these were greatly enlarged. They stood in the centre of the city, but later the brothers' convent was moved to the suburb of Montmusart where it was generally known as the *auberge*. It included communal dormitories and individual cells. The hospice for poor pilgrims was given a tall fortified tower. It stood near the city wall, separated from the fortified Palace of the Master by a road. The palace was a mixture of administrative offices and conventual buildings, though the Order probably used part of their fortified headquarters as a prison for disorderly brothers. A great deal of the Hospitaller complex in Acre survives to this day, including what was probably the refectory with three chimneys and a kitchen next door. The original structure probably also included the hospice or inn for pilgrims and newly arrived brothers, plus a church and the *domus infirmorum*, a hospital in the modern sense.

Hospitallers' infirmaries were remarkable institutions, that in Jerusalem being a large and beautiful building, over 75 metres long, 40 metres wide, with tall arches. It could also accommodate up to 1,000 patients. In fact the Hospitaller hospital in Jerusalem was so widely respected that, when he liberated Jerusalem, Saladin allowed the Order

Although medical science in Western Europe was more backward than in the Islamic world, the Europeans were not as primitive as once thought. This textbook for surgeons was based upon lecture notes from the medical school of Salerno. Above, left: using forceps to flatten the barbs of an arrow before removing it. Above, right: stitching a wound caused by an edged weapon. (Guido of Arezzo's *Chirurgia*)

a full year to bring its work to an orderly close and transfer those patients who were too sick to be moved immediately.

The Hospitaller *domus infirmorum* in Acre was also called the Palais des Malades. Its remains still stand and consist of six parallel halls opening onto a sunlit courtyard. The basic structure was, in fact, the northern part of a large Islamic *khan* or merchant's 'motel' dating from the 10th-11th century to which the Hospitallers added further floors. Another Hospitaller hospital existed at Mont Pélerin where excavations uncovered two adjacent churches with a shared passage within the wall. No building could be identified as the *domus infirmorum* so this may have been upstairs, over the twin chapels and reached by the passage and stairs.

The conventual life of the Hospitallers was governed by a Rule compiled by the second Master, Raymond de Puy, and was based upon poverty, chastity, obedience, eating and sleeping communally. A daily routine revolved around the monastic *horarium* or 'hours', all brothers attending religious services. Many brothers were illiterate and so were expected merely to listen and say *paternosters* (the Lord's Prayer in Latin) for each section of the religious day. Brothers away on business or at war were similarly expected to say a certain number of *paternosters*. Each brother also had to attend Holy Communion at least three times a year at Christmas, Easter and Pentecost. Prayers for the sick were recited every evening by Hospitaller brother-chaplains or priests from outside the Order.

The brethren went to bed after the service of Compline and rose for the service of Matins. They had to be silent in the dormitories, were forbidden to sleep naked despite the Middle Eastern heat, nor could they share beds in cold winters, while a candle was always burning in the dormitory. By the 1170s these rules were changed for senior men who soon acquired their own private rooms or cells.

Eating was supposedly communal, though some men again obtained the right to eat alone in their cells. Most monks were prohibited from

LEFT the so-called Crypt of St John was the refectory of the Hospitallers' Central Convent in Acre. (Israel Press Information Office photograph) RIGHT a carved fleurs-de-lys in this refectory might reflect the fact that Louis VII of France offered to pay for the building while he was in Acre. (Z. Goldman photograph)

eating the meat of four-footed animals and at first this applied to the Hospitallers, but the rule was gradually relaxed, particularly when brothers were on campaign and needed to keep up their strength. There was a similar increase in the allowance of 'pittances' of extra food and drink under certain circumstances. The fasts which the Hospitallers observed were less than those endured by ordinary monks, and most were in winter rather than the summer campaigning season. In fact there was concern to stop over-enthusiastic brothers fasting too much as this could undermine military effectiveness. Even the rule against talking while eating was more lenient on campaign. Nor was it always obeyed, as there were complaints about rowdy brothers beating servants who brought the food, or pelting them with pieces of bread.

In the eyes of their contemporaries, the Hospitallers ate quite well. They were summoned to the refectory by a bell twice a day, each meal usually having two sittings – the second was for those on duty during the first. In 1206 the first meal was before the religious service of Nones, the second after Vespers and no wine was drunk after Compline. The staple diet consisted of cooked meats, fish, eggs, bread and wine – and this had to be good enough to be 'stomached'. In periods of abstinence they gave up meat. In Lent they drank no milk and there were no eggs or cheese on Fridays. Such rules were relaxed at sea and additional pittances, especially of wine, became more common during the 13th century. After a meal the brethren rose and went to say grace in the church.

In Western Europe their work largely revolved around farming, charitable or medical duties, but in the Middle East military training probably took up much of the brothers' remaining time and was mostly carried out in the afternoon, probably because of the heat. Later evidence suggests that only three days a week were dedicated to military exercises such as gymnastics, wrestling, assorted drill, exercises in arms and crossbow shooting. Other evidence about military training is negative and indicated what a brother-in-arms was not permitted to do, namely hunting, hawking and taking part in tournaments. A further statute banned the carrying or drawing of the *arcus de bondec*, or pellet-bow, in town. Nor were men allowed to gallop their horses unless ordered to do so by their *bailli*.

The maintenance of discipline was central to the Order's existence. However, accusations that a brother had broken the Rule could only be made before a chapter or council meeting. If a brother complained publicly before privately telling another of his error, or if he denounced a brother outside the chapter, he himself could be subject to the same punishment as the 'slandered' man. The result was a complicated and often prolonged system of internal justice. Once an individual decided to make a complaint the legal system became very formal and the resulting *esgart* consisted of three parts: a formal *plaint*, the hearing of evidence, and the decision by chapter. A fourth stage could be an appeal to higher authority. Witnesses were interrogated in the presence of both parties, and resulting punishments were similar to those of other religious orders. The most lenient was to be denied cooked food or wine which could be imposed by a community without recourse to a full chapter. In Syria it was imposed for misdemeanours such as misbehaving at meals, laziness or being disorderly in the *auberge*. Next came a series of penances. More serious were the *septaine* or seven days 'loss of habit'

The production and export of sugar was a major source of income in the Crusader States. This structure near where the Wadi Rajab joins the Jordan valley is believed to have been part of a medieval sugar crushing mill. (Carl Andrews photograph)

and *quarantaine*, 40 days 'loss of habit', while the most serious penalty was expulsion from the Order.

The most important of the Hospitallers' non-military duties were tending the sick and injured. A large section of the Order's *Old French Rule* was entitled: 'Concerning food for the sick and doctors and the organisation of the palace of the sick in Jerusalem.' Here the organisation of the *infirmorum* was different from that in the more complex hospitals of the Islamic and Byzantine worlds. Wards in the Palace of the Sick were not divided into specialised sections, for example. However, the *Old French Rule* specified in detail how the hospital's income should be used, including the purchase of almonds for the sick at Easter and at the Feast of the Holy Cross. The Rule similarly explained the admissions procedure, how each new patient was allocated to a specific sergeant, and how a newcomer's possessions were placed in safe keeping, along with the daily routine of staff and patients.

Surgeons were regarded as *practici*, practical men set slightly apart from the higher status physicians, the *theorici* who dealt with diet, herbal medicines and the analysis of a patient's urine. Surgeons also operated first-aid stations near a scene of battle. The wounded were then brought back to Jerusalem, on the brother-knights' horses if nothing else was available. In the hospital they were treated by physicians, surgeons and blood-letters. For example, after the battle of Montgisard in 1177,

ABOVE **The massive Hospitaller castle of Krak des Chevaliers looming over a vital pass linking the Mediterranean to the Syrian interior. (Author's photograph)**

OPPOSITE **The battle of Gaza in 1239 was a major blow to the Crusader States and sent shock waves across Western Europe. Here, the shields of three leaders are shown upside down along with the similarly upturned banners of the Hospitallers (left) and Templars (right). (*Historia Anglorum*, British Library, Ms. Roy. 14.CVII, f.130v, London, England)**

750 wounded men were taken to the hospital which already contained 900 sick people.

The doctors were not themselves members of the Hospitaller Order. In 1182 the hospital in Jerusalem required four doctors capable of examining urine, diagnosing diseases and prescribing medicines. Jerusalem had become a renowned medical centre, with physicians coming from Europe and the Middle East to work there. Many disapproved of employing non-Christian doctors or of using advanced Middle Eastern medical knowledge and there was clear rivalry between physicians of different faiths. But whatever their background, physicians and surgeons who wanted to practise in the Crusader States had to pass a verbal examination.

Less is known about those who served as nurses. According to the *Old French Rule* there were 12 sergeants to each ward, their duties being to make the beds, keep them clean and to help the sick or injured to the toilet. Two brothers were similarly on duty each night. Sisters of the Hospitaller Order may have helped tend the sick in the early days, although this is unlikely, and in later years Hospitaller sisters led an enclosed, contemplative life. The women who did work in the hospital were probably paid servants of the Order. Female patients were clearly treated in Hospitaller hospitals and were mentioned in the very early Anglo-Norman version of the *Rule*, where it was specified that new-born babies should sleep in cots separate from their mothers.

When the brothers fell sick they were excused ordinary duties and fasts, but not punishment. The master could give permission for aged or infirm brethren-in-arms to hand in their military equipment, while those who became lepers had to live separately with fellow sufferers, although they were still fed and clothed by the Order. A brother also had to get permission before being bled for medical reasons as this caused temporary weakness. The most sick were moved to a conventual infirmary which was separate from the conventual buildings, but close to the church. A man's bed and weaponry would be taken to the infirmary where he confessed his sins, stated whether he was a debtor or creditor, or had possessions of his own. An inventory of his goods was made, he was given the sacraments and handed over any keys of office to his prior. Once in the infirmary a patient was forbidden to play chess, read romances or eat prohibited food. Nevertheless a special refectory was attached to the infirmary, serving a wider choice of food and a better wine.

Complex regulations governed what happened when a brother of the Order died. In the late 12th century the body was laid out before burial and the flag of the Order was draped over the bier which, surrounded by candles, was watched over while priests chanted psalms. After 1278 brothers were buried in their mantles and all brothers had to attend the service unless ordered elsewhere. Each year the anniversary of a brother's death was commemorated in his convent's calendar. The *Rule* also stated that 30 masses should be said for each dead brother, while priests read from the Psalter as lay brothers said 150 *paternosters*. In the Central Convent in Jerusalem five priests similarly read the Psalter every evening for the souls of the Order's benefactors. On the first Sunday in Lent a solemn requiem mass was also conducted for the souls of deceased Masters and brethren.

COLOUR PLATE COMMENTARY

A: KNIGHT AND SERGEANT UNIFORMS

1: Brother-in-arms, c.1160. In addition to an undecorated iron helmet and a mail coif, the brother-at-arms is protected by a mail hauberk. His monk's black cappa has a simple cross sewn to the breast. His large leather-covered wooden shield is undecorated except for a painted cross, as is his sword, scabbard and horse-harness. This was the ideal of 'simplicity' which the Hospitallers attempted to maintain for several centuries.

2: Brother sergeant-at-arms, c.1250. Apart from some modernisation in his arms and armour, the main change in this man's appearance is the abandonment of a cappa for a black surcoat. The cross on the surcoat is also of the eight-pointed type which became a Hospitaller's badge. His armour consists of an early cervellière helmet worn beneath a mail coif, a hauberk with one integral mitten, a quilted gambeson beneath this hauberk, and mail chausses on his legs. He holds a brother knight's horse which is covered by a quilted caparison with a chamfron to protect its head. There is also a small heraldic escutcheon on its saddle, which was allowed at this time.

3: Brother knight-at-arms, c.1275. By the 1270s the Pope permitted Hospitallers to use different coloured surcoats to distinguish brother-knights from brother-sergeants. Shown here is a quilted version with short sleeves, probably known as a jupell. To support his almost flat-topped great-helm, he has a leather arming cap with a padded squab around the brows. The mittens of his mail hauberk are thrown back to his wrists, he has a modern form of buckled sword-belt and iron poleyns are attached to quilted cuisses to protect his knees.

4: Brother knight-at-arms, c.1305. The red surcoat or partially padded jupon was now worn by all Hospitaller brethren-at-arms. There is also a strongly Italian influence in this man's armour, ranging from his one-piece, deep-brimmed war-hat to the jupon itself, the dagger hung from his belt, and the hardened leather greaves over the mail chausses on his legs. He also wears an unusual form of fabric-covered scale cuirass plus comparable gauntlets. These are based on an effigy of a northern Italian knight who is believed to have been a member of a Military Order.

B: TREATING WOUNDED IN THE HOSPITAL, EARLY 12TH CENTURY

The wards of the domus infirmorum in Jerusalem could get crowded after a battle when injured men would be added to the long-term sick already there. Yet the number of physicians, surgeons and Hospitaller brother-sergeants on duty remained small. There would, however, have been a larger number of paid servants, and in times of crisis other brothers would presumably have helped. The methods used to treat war-injuries in the 12th century are illustrated in a number of sometimes graphic manuscript illustrations, as reconstructed here.

C: ARMS AND ARMOUR C.1140

This knight wears a one-piece iron helmet (1), that has leather chin-straps (2) and a nasal made from a separate piece of iron (3). Beneath the helmet is a padded mail coif. His outermost layer, a broad and loose-fitting monk's cappa of black cloth, has a very large hood, and is tapered with a white cord worn around the waist. Note also how the left side of the cappa has been gathered up over the sword and scabbard so that the weapon can be drawn. Beneath this he wears a mail hauberk (4), slit at the front and back, with long hems and broad untailored sleeves. Under the hauberk, mostly hidden from view, is a stiff, quilted aketon (5), whose half-length sleeves would 'bulge' the shape of the black cappa around the elbows. Beneath the aketon he wears a long, white linen tunic. On his feet are soft leather shoes (6), under which are cotton hose. Attached to his feet are plain iron spurs (7).

The hauberk is shown laid out (4), with an integral mail coif (8). The mail ventail (9), a flap used to protect the lower face and chin, is shown hanging open and 'untied'. The interior of the largely unlined coif is also shown, together with the linen-covered padding in the skull (10). Note the slit in the left side of the hauberk for the sword hilt (11), and how the hems are split at the front and back to facilitate movement. The padded aketon is also shown laid flat (5). It has leather edging around the sleeves, neck and hem (12): it has vertical stitching in doubled rows; and horizontal stitching in single rows. It has a rectangular neck opening, and a rectangular slit in the front and back of the hem. Note also that at the armpits it has an unquilted filet (13).

He carries an iron-headed spear (14), which has a plain wooden haft: also shown is a detail of the cross-section of the head (15). His sword (16) has a leather-covered wooden grip (16a), and an undecorated, disc-shaped iron pommel (16b) and quillons (16c). It has a gold cross inlaid in the blade (16d), and a fuller-groove down the blade, which can be seen more clearly in the cross-section detail (16e).

The scabbard (17) is made of wood and covered in leather, with a copper chape at the base (18), a detail of which is shown (19). It is attached by a knotted leather sword-belt. Two details of the top of the scabbard are shown: the first shows the leather sleeve around which the belt laces or straps are tied (20), and the second shows the rear of this, with the straps attached (21).

He also bears a shield. This is of wooden construction and covered in leather, with an iron boss in the middle on the front. The interior of the shield with its vertical 'keel' shape is shown (22). It has a leather guige with an iron buckle (23) for securing it across the shoulder and chest, a leather covered padded squab (24), and hand straps (25): these are secured with rivets and rings (26). Also shown is a section through the centre of the shield (27).

D: DEFENDING PILGRIMS C.1150

The Hospitallers were created to care for sick or injured pilgrims in the Holy Land, but they were soon involved in protecting those who wanted to visit isolated or dangerous shrines. The threat came not only from bandits but from semi-official raiders at a time when the frontiers of the Crusader States remained vulnerable. Here a group of pilgrims have been ambushed by raiders from the isolated Fatimid Egyptian garrison at Ascalon which finally fell to the kingdom of Jerusalem in 1153.

E: CLOTHING ALLOCATION ACCORDING TO THE HOSPITALLER STATUTE OF 1206

1: White linen or cotton breeches (x 3 pairs).
2: White linen or cotton shirt (x 3).
3: Linen cotta (x 3).
4: White hose (x 2 pairs, one linen, one wool).
5: Cotton coif (x 1).
6: White cap, probably of felt (x 1).
7: Black woollen garnache and hood (x 1).
8: Black woollen mantle lined with fur for winter (x 1).
9: Black woollen mantle, unlined for summer (x 1).
10: White linen bedding sheets (x 4).
11: Linen bag for bedding (x 1).

F: CARAVAN RAID C.1250

The Hospitallers not only provided local expertise when Crusader forces launched a raid against neighbouring Islamic territory. They also provided some of the most disciplined units. The regulations which governed the behaviour of brethren-at-arms on active service were highly detailed and specified when men could drink or water their horses. Here, a unit of Hospitallers is on a raid, but they are having trouble maintaining discipline amongst non-Hospitaller troops and European Crusaders, some of the latter having broken ranks to drink at a spring.

G: ARMS AND ARMOUR C.1230

The knight wears a fluted iron helmet with a face-mask riveted to the front. Next to this is shown the quilted linen coif (1), which was worn under a separate mail coif (2): the mail coif has leather edging around face, and the mail ventail is shown laced at the left temple. Note the rectangular lower outline of the coif. On top of the mail coif is a padded leather squab for the helmet (3), and also worn is a leather brow-band tied at the back of the head (4). The helmet is also shown in front view (5).

His outer layer is a heavy woollen cappa, with a large hood and broad, long sleeves: there are no slits in the hem. Sewn to the front of this is the new style of cross, and tied around the waist is a white rope. The long sleeves of the cappa are partially rolled back.

Beneath the cappa he wears a linen covered, quilted, sleeveless gambeson (6): the collar is secured by wooden buttons and leather loops. A narrow leather belt with an iron buckle tapers it to the body.

Beneath this he wears a long-sleeved mail hauberk (7) with integral mittens (8) but no coif. At the front of the neck is an overlapping opening for added protection. The mittens have a soft leather palm, which are slit sideways. Note also the laces for tightening the wrists of the hauberk, these were probably attached permanently. Under the hauberk he wears a quilted cotton covered aketon (9).

His legs are protected on the front by mail chausses (10), kept up by a knotted leather suspender to a narrow leather belt around the waist. On his feet, inside the chausses, are leather shoes (11). Around his middle leg are plain soft leather quilted cuisses (12): these are laced around the upper and lower edges. Beneath the chausses are linen hose (13) kept up by leather laces, and under these he wears cotton breeches (14), with a drawstring around the waist.

One of his weapons is a single-edged faussar-type weapon (15) with a wooden grip. This is also shown in an

BELOW **The half round tower which forms the corner of the outer wall of Marqab was rebuilt by Sultan Qala'un after he captured the castle in 1285, but behind is the main keep erected by the Hospitallers. (Author's photograph)**

His shield (20) is wood covered in leather: in this form of shield the internal nails cannot be seen on the front. It has a leather guige with iron buckle (21), for attachment over the shoulder, and a padded leather squab (22). Note that only two of the inner straps over the squab are buckled.

H: A MEETING OF THE CHAPTER C.1270
This gathering is taking place in the Hospitaller castle of Krak des Chevaliers. There were strict regulations about not carrying arms or wearing armour in chapter, presumably to avoid intimidation. A 'non-brother' sergeant is present to maintain order and is evicting an over-enthusiastic petitioner. Nearby, a brother-sergeant is passing a petition to the Conventual Prior, while the Brother Cellarer, distinguished by his bunch of keys, listens.

I: THE BANNER OF THE ORDER OF THE HOSPITAL OF ST JOHN AND THE COATS OF ARMS OF ITS MASTERS TO 1306
The supposed coats-of-arms of the earliest masters were drawn up in later years in the belief that such notable men must have had them. Other early arms are similarly unreliable, having been based upon those used by families claiming some association with the families of the first masters. This illustration also shows a Hospitaller standard bearer from c. 1260.

1: The Blessed Gerard (1099-1120)
2: The Blessed Raymond du Puy (1120-60)
3: Auger de Balben (1160-62)
4: Arnold de Comps (1162)
5: Gilbert d'Assailly (1162-70)
6: Cast de Murols (1170-72)
7: Jobert de Syrie (1172-77)
8: Roger de Moulins (1177-87)
9: Armengaud d'Asp (1188-90)
10: Garnier de Naples (1190-92)
11: Geoffrey de Donjon (1193-1202)
12: Alfonso de Portugal (1203-06)
13: Geoffrey le Rat (1206-07)
14: Garin de Montaigu (1207-28)
15: Bertrand de Thessy (1228-30)
16: Guerin (1230-36)
17: Bertrand de Comps (1236-39)
18: Pierre de Vieille Bride (1239-42)
19: Guillaume de Châteauneuf (1242-58)
20: Hugues Revel (1258-77)
21: Nicholas Lorgne (1277-85)
22: Jean de Villiers (1285-93)
23: Eudes des Pins (1293-96)
24: Guillaume de Villaret (1296-1305) and Foulques de Villaret (1305-1319)

J: THE FALL OF ACRE, 1291
The Hospitallers, the Templars and the Teutonic Knights played a heroic role in the final defence of Acre but the Hospitallers emerged from this disaster with the greatest credit, partly because they were more successful in helping refugees to escape from the doomed city. There must have been terror and chaos in Acre's narrow streets, particularly near the harbour, as panic-stricken people tried to get aboard the few ships available to carry them to safety.

ABOVE **Most of Acre was rebuilt following the end of the crusader occupation. Nevertheless part of a Frankish tower still stands at the end of a wharf built on top of the medieval quay. (Author's photograph)**

'exploded' view. He also bears an undecorated iron sword with a hazelnut-shaped pommel (16). When not in use this is carried in a scabbard (17) attached to a slit and knotted sword-belt: both the front view and a rear view (18) of the lacing system of the sword-belt to the scabbard is shown. Also shown is an example and detail of tooled decoration for the front of the leather-covered wooden scabbard (19).

COLLECTIONS AND MAJOR RELATED SITES

The Middle East and parts of Europe are dotted with castles associated with the Hospitallers. Those in the Holy Land and neighbouring regions are listed below. As one of the largest, richest and most powerful trans-national organisations in the medieval world, the Order of the Hospitallers left a huge number of documents and elaborate seals which are preserved in archives throughout Europe. The Order also still exists in different forms ranging from the St John's Ambulance Brigade to the Roman Catholic Sovereign Military Order of St John and four non-Catholic Orders of St John in Germany, Sweden, the Netherlands and the United Kingdom. These are, perhaps, the finest 'relics' of all.

Archives and Museums

Malta: National Library, Valetta, incorporating the archives of the Order of St John.
England: Museum of the Order of St John, London, which includes a small museum and excellent library.

Main Middle Eastern Castles

Cyprus: Paphos, incomplete castle.
Israel: Arsuf, ruined castle and town; Ascalon, ruins of city wall; Bayt Jibrin, ruins of fortification; Belvoir, ruined castle; Mount Tabor, ruined fortifications; Qalansuwa, remains of fortified tower.
Lebanon: Akkar, ruins of castle.
Syria: (excluding numerous minor castles): Jableh, remains of fortified town; Krak des Chevaliers, complete castle; Marqab, almost complete castle; Qala'at Banu Israil, ruined castle; Qala'at Yahmur, almost complete small castle.
Turkey: Silifke, ruined castle; Toprak-kale; ruined castle.

The church in Bahdeidat in Lebanon contains the largest surviving Crusader-period wall paintings in the country. Surviving fragments in Hospitaller chapels suggest that they were decorated in a similar manner. (In situ church, Bahdeidat, Lebanon; E. Cruikshank-Dodd photograph)

BIBLIOGRAPHY

Balard, M., (edit.) *Autour de la Premiere Croisade,* Paris 1996

Barber, M.C., (edit.) *The Military Orders; Fighting for the Faith and Caring for the Sick,* Aldershot 1994

Cagnin, G., *Templari e Giovanniti in Territorio Trevigiano (secoli XII-XIV),* Treviso 1992

Coli, E., (et al. edits.) *Militia Sacra, Gli Ordini militari tra Europe e Terrasanta* Perugia 1994

Constable, G., *Monks, Crusaders and Hermits in Medieval Europe,* London 1988

Delaville le Roulx, J.M.A. (edit.) *Cartulaire Générale de l'Ordre des Hospitaliers de St Jean de Jérusalem,* Paris 1894-1906

Delaville le Roulx, J.M.A., *Les Hospitaliers en Terre Sainte et a Chypre 1100-1310* Paris 1904

Demurger, A., *Les ordres religieux-militaires de la premiere croisade à Lepante,* Paris 1999

Dobronic, L., 'The Military Orders in Croatia,' in V.P. Goss (edit.), *The Meeting of Two World, Cultural Exchange between East and West during the Period of the Crusades,* Kalamazoo 1986

Edgington, S., 'The Hospital of St John in Jerusalem,' in Z. Amar (et al edits.), *Medicine in Jerusalem throughout the Ages,* Jerusalem 1997

Favreau-Lilie. M-L., 'The Military Orders and the Escape of the Christian Population from the Holy Land in 1291,' *Journal of Medieval History* XIX (1993)

Forey, A.J., 'Gli ordini militari e la difesa degli stati crociati,' in Balletto, L. (edit.), *Oriente e Occidente tra medioevo ed eta moderna - studi in honore G. Pistarino,* Genoa 1997.

Forey, A.J., *Military Orders and Crusaders,* London 1994

Forey, A.J., *The Military Orders from the Twelfth to the early Fourteenth Centuries,* London 1991

Goldmann, Z., *Akko in the Time of the Crusades, The Convent of the Order of St John,* (Jerusalem 1994).

Harot, E., *Essai d'Armorial des Grands Maitres de l'Ordre de St Jean de Jérusalem,* Rome 1911

Hiestand, R., 'Castrum peregrinorum e la fine del domino crociato in Siria,' in *La fine della presenza degli ordini militari e Terra Santa e i nuovi orientamenti nel XIVs,* Perugia 1996

Hunt, T., *The Medieval Surgery,* Woodbridge 1992

Kedar, B.Z., (et al edits.), *Outremer: Studies in the History of the Crusading Kingdom of Jerusalem Presented to Joshua Prawern,* Jerusalem 1982.

Kedar, B.Z., *The Franks in the Levant, 11th to 14th centuries,* London 1993

Kennedy, H., *Crusader Castles,* London 1994

King, E.J., *The Knights Hospitaller in the Holy Land,* London 1931

King, E.J., *The Rules, Statutes and Customs of the Hospitallers 1099-1310,* London 1934

Lacroix, P., *La Chevalerie et les Croisades, Feodalite-Blason-Ordres Militaires,* Paris 1890

Ligato, G., 'Il Magister Ospidaliero Ruggero des Moulins neela Crisi Finale del Regno Latino di Gerusalemme (1182-1187),' *Antoniarum* LXXI, 1996

Luttrell, A., 'The Earliest Hospitallers,' in B.Z. Kedar (et al edits.), *Montjoie: Studies in Crusade History in Honour of Hand Eberhard Mayer,* Aldershot 1997

Luttrell, A., *The Hospitallers in Cyprus, Rhodes, Greece and the West (1291-1440),* London 1978

'Militia Christi' e Crociata nei secoli XI-XIII: Attil della XI Settimana internazionale di Studio, Mendola 28 agosto-1 settembre 1989, *Miscellanea del Centro di studi medievali,* Vol. III, Milan 1992

Mitchell, P.D., 'Surgery in the Crusades,' *St John Historical Society Proceedings,* 1997

Nicholson, H.J., *Templars, Hospitallers and Teutonic Knights: Images of the Military Orders 1128-1291,* Leicester 1993

Nicholson, H.J. (edit.), *The Military Orders, Volume 2. Welfare and Warfare,* Cardiff 1998

Phillips, J., *Defenders of the Holy Land: Relations between the Latin East and the West, 1119-1187,* 1996

Pringle, R.D., 'Crusader Castles: The First Generation,' *Fortress,* I, 1989

Restagno, J.C., (edit.), *Cavalieri di San Giovanni e Territorio,* Borgighera 1999

Riley-Smith, J., *Hospitallers: The History of the Order of St John,* London 1999

Riley-Smith, J., *The Knights of St John in Jerusalem and Cyprus, c.1050-1310,* London 1967

Sarnowsky, J. (edit.), *Mendicants, Military Orders and Regionalism in Medieval Europe,* Aldershot 1999

Schatzmiller, M., (edit.), *Crusaders and Muslims in Twelfth Century Syria,* Leiden 1993

Sinclair, K.V., The Hospitallers' Riwle. Miracula et Regula Hospitalis Sancti Johannis Jerosolimitani, *Anglo-Norman Texts,* Vol. 42, London 1984

Wienand, A. (edit.), *Der Johanniter Orden: Der Malteser Orden: Der ritterliche Orden des hl. Johannes vom Spital zu Jerusalem: Seine Aufgaben, seine Geschichte,* Cologne 1970

Williams, A., 'Crusaders as Frontiersmen: The Case of the Order of St John in the Mediterranean,' in D. Power and N. Standen (edits.), *Frontiers in Questions: Eurasian Borderlands 700-1700,* Basingstoke 1999

GLOSSARY

Afeutreüre: perhaps an early form of soft-armour.
Arbalestry: crossbow-store.
Arcus de bondec: pellet bow.
Auberc jaserant: fabric-covered and padded mail hauberk.
Bailli: title of executive administrative authority.
Baldric: shoulder strap to carry a scabbard.
Barding: horse coverings or armour.
Bascinet: close fitting helmet.
Bataille: battlefield division.
Biretta: hat.
Brother of the parmentarie: brother-in-service assisting the Drapier.
Brother-at-arms: member of a Military Order having military duties.
Brother-at-service: member of a Military Order having non-military duties.
Capitular bailli: senior bailli.
Cappa: monastic habit.
Caravanier: another name for brother-sergeants-at-arms.
Casal: village estate.
Castellan: officer in command of an important castle.
Chapel de fer: brimmed helmet.
Chapter: meeting of a convent or of the executive members of a religious order.
Charger: warhorse.
Chauses avantpiés: hose incorporating pointed toes.
Chausses: mail leg protections.
Commander of Knights: officer who led the knights if the marshal or his lieutenant were not available.
Commander of the Vault: official in charge of stores.
Commander: officer in charge of a Hospitaller commandery.
Commandery: territorial division of the Hospitaller Order.
Confrater: layman associated with the Hospitallers.
Conrois: tactical cavalry unit.
Constable: senior organizational military officer.
Conventual bailli: official or bailli in the Central Convent.
Conventual Prior: the Order's most senior religious official.
Coreaus de fetur: leather cuirass.

Cotes hardie: short coat.
Cotta: tunic.
Coutel: dagger.
Crie: official who ran the stables.
Cuirasses: leather body armour.
Cuirie: leather body armour.
Cuisses: quilted protection for the thighs.
Destrier: warhorse.
Domus: house, or small Hospitaller convent.
Donat: noblemen waiting to join the Hospitallers as a full brother.
Drapier: official in charge of clothing.
Eschiell: cavalry squadron.
Esgart: legal complaint and judgement.
Espalier d'arme: mail or padded shoulder defence.
Estiveaus: boots.
Faussar affilé: unclear form of infantry weapon with a long blade.
Galoches: large overshoes.
Garnache: hooded coat
General Chapter: governing committee of the Order.
Gipelle: jupon or quilted soft armour.
Gonfanier: standard-bearer.
Gonfanon: glag.
Grand Commander: master's administrative second in command.
Grand Esquire: officer in charge of the Master's own squires.
Guisarme d'acier: long-hafted infantry axe.
Hargan: long coat.
Hauberk: basic mail armour for the body and arms.
Horarium: sequence of daily religious services in a monastic order.
Hospice: hostel, often for pilgrims.
Hospitaller: official responsible for the sick.
Manicle de fer: integral mail mitten.
Manumission: the freeing of a serf by his lord.
Marshal: the most senior military official in the Order.
Marshalsy: department run by the marshal.
Master esquire: a senior brother-sergeant of the Central Convent in charge of squires, grooms and stables.
Master: the senior figure in the Hospitaller Order.

Mêlée: close combat, often after a charge.
Ministeriales: warriors with the legal status of serfs but otherwise forming a military elite, mostly in Germany.
Misericorde: dagger.
Novitiate: system of training youngsters for possible entry into a religious order.
Oblation: the placing of boys in a religious order for their education.
Oreillet: form of hat covering the ears.
Panceriam: lighter or more limited form of mail armour.
Parmentarie: clothing store and tailoring department.
Pennoncelle: small pennon.
Planeaus: sandals.
Playines: plate armour.
Points: laces to which hose and other garments could be attached.
Priory: administrative province of the Hospitaller Order.
Quarantaine: punishment of 40 days 'loss of habit.'
Rondel: perhaps a type of scarf.
Septaine: punishment of seven days 'loss of habit.'
Serf: European of unfree status but not a slave.
Simony: the purchase of ecclesiastical positions.
Soliers: ordinary shoes.
Soubre seignal: perhaps a surcoat.
Statute: ruling by the Central Chapter of the Order.
Sub-Marshal: assistant to the marshal.
Surcoat: loose garment worn over armour.
Talevas: large infantry shield or mantlet.
Treasurer: official in charge of the Treasury.
Turcopole: soldier of Middle Eastern origin serving in the forces of the Crusader States in his traditional manner.
Turcopolier: officer in command of Turcopoles.
Usance: custom or tradition of the Order.
Ventail: mail flap to protect throat and chin.

INDEX